Wild about Cupcakes

Wild about Cupcakes

Rachel Lane

BARRON'S

First English language edition
for the United States and Canada
published in 2009 by Barron's Educational Series, Inc.

Originally published under the title *Wild About Cupcakes*
Copyright © McRae Books Srl 2009

Wild About Cupcakes
was created and produced by McRae Books Srl
Via del Salviatino, 1 – 50016 Fiesole, Florence, Italy
info@mcraebooks.com
www.mcraebooks.com
Publishers: Anne McRae, Marco Nardi

Project Director Anne McRae
Art Director Marco Nardi
Photography Brent Parker Jones, Paul Nelson (R&R PhotoStudio)
Introduction Carla Bardi
Texts Rachel Lane
Food Styling Lee Blaylock, Michelle Finn
Stylist Lee Blaylock
Food Preparation Rebecca Quinn, Michelle Finn
Layouts Aurora Granata
Pre-press Filippo Delle Monache, Davide Gasparri
Cover design Marco Nardi

All inquiries should be addressed to:
Barron's Educational Series, Inc.
250 Wireless Boulevard
Hauppauge, New York 11788
www.barronseduc.com

ISBN-13: 978-0-7641-6277-0
ISBN-10: 0-7641-6277-2

Library of Congress Control Number: 2009923825

Printed in China
9 8 7 6 5 4 3 2 1

The level of difficulty for each recipe is given on a scale from
1 (easy) to 3 (complicated).

CONTENTS

INTRODUCTION

Cupcakes, or fairy cakes as they are also known, especially in Britain, are thought to have originated in North America in the early 19th century when it became usual to bake using a cup to measure out the ingredients. In the same way that pound cakes contained a pound each of various ingredients, cupcakes may have been made from a sequence of cup measures. But these tiny cakes were also baked in small pottery molds or cups and it may have been this fact that gave rise to the name.

Whatever the origin of the name, perhaps it is the British expression—fairy cakes—that best captures the spirit of these diminutive treats. Temptingly tiny and exquisitely decorated, like their namesakes they are always a joy to behold. What's more, most cupcakes are not tremendously difficult to make.

In this book we have selected 130 recipes for cupcakes for every occasion—all of which can easily be prepared at home. We have graded each recipe 1, 2, or 3 for level of difficulty, with most falling into the first or second categories. There are a few more challenging recipes, for those of you who want to test your baking skills!

The recipes are divided into five chapters; the first features healthy and simple cupcakes that can be made easily and quickly and served for breakfast, brunch, or snacks. The second chapter is entirely dedicated to chocolate, with 28 scrumptious recipes to please chocolate lovers. Chapter three focuses on cupcakes that children will enjoy, both to eat and to help prepare. The fourth chapter features party themes, with recipes for birthday, Christmas, Easter, Halloween, and New Year cupcakes, among others. The final chapter has recipes for those "special moments," from bridal showers to wedding days, and from golden anniversaries to graduations and Mother's Day.

SPECIAL DIETARY NEEDS

Throughout the book you will also find that some of the recipes are marked with symbols for those with special health needs. These are:

Apricot & Ginger Cupcakes, p. 78
Chocolate & Pecan Cupcakes, p. 92
Chocolate and Walnut Mud Cupcakes, p. 120
Chocolate and Strawberry Cupcakes, p. 142
Toadstool Cupcakes, p. 172

Independence Day Cupcakes, p. 236
Birthday Cupcakes, p. 240
Chocolate Decadence Cupcakes, p. 248
Chocolate Love Cupcakes, p. 262
Mother's Day Cupcakes, p. 280

Apricot & Ginger Cupcakes, p. 78
Coconut Butterfly Cupcakes, p. 156
For My Sweetheart Cupcakes, p. 260

Baby Doll Cupcakes, p. 268
Independence Day Cupcakes, p. 236

Granny's Apple Cupcakes, p. 74
Chocolate Cupcakes, p. 82
Chocolate & Macadamia cupcakes, p. 114
Chocolate Berry Cupcakes, p. 126

Traffic Light Cupcakes, p. 148
Chocolate Berry Creams Cupcakes, p. 180
Chocolate Mint Bunny Cupcakes, p. 228
Graduation Hat Cupcakes, p. 272

Blueberry Swirl Cupcakes, p. 24
Chocolate Cupcakes, p. 82

Bananas In Pajamas Cupcakes, p. 164
Chocolate Berry Creams Cupcakes, p. 180

Plum & Pecan Cupcakes, p. 28
Pear & Oat Cupcakes, p. 36
Apricot Cupcakes, p. 42

Banana and Yogurt Cupcakes, p. 64
Banana Split Cupcakes, p. 146
Orange Swirls Cupcakes, p. 200

Follow these recipes and you can prepare cupcakes for yourself, or for friends and family with food allergies or who are diabetic. A word of warning about preparing food for people with food allergies: always carefully read the labels of all ingredients to make sure there are not traces of the food that you are seeking to avoid. For example, some types of chocolate and vanilla extract (essence) contain gluten which could make a person suffering from celiac disease very ill. When preparing food for people with special health needs you are best advised to buy high quality products from reputable companies that specialize in manufacturing these foods. They can be found at natural food stores.

simple &
healthy

1	cup (150 g) rhubarb, cut in ½-inch (1-cm) dice	1	teaspoon baking powder
2	tablespoons water	⅛	teaspoon salt
3	tablespoons light brown sugar	½	cup (125 g) unsalted butter, softened
½	vanilla bean, split lengthways and seeds scraped out	½	cup (100 g) sugar
		2	large eggs
1¼	cups (180 g) all-purpose (plain) flour	½	cup (125 ml) milk Confectioners' (icing) sugar, to dust

RHUBARB & VANILLA CUPCAKES

Preheat the oven to 325°F (170°C/gas 3).
• Line a standard 12-cup muffin tin with paper liners. • Stew the rhubarb with the water, brown sugar, and vanilla pod and seeds in a small saucepan over low heat until softened, 5–10 minutes. Discard the vanilla pod. Set aside to cool. • Combine the flour, baking powder, and salt in a small bowl. • Beat the butter and sugar in a medium bowl with an electric mixer on medium-high speed until pale and creamy. • Add the eggs one at a time, beating until just blended after each addition.
• With mixer on low speed, add the mixed dry ingredients alternating, with the milk. • Stir the rhubarb in by hand. • Spoon the batter into the prepared cups, filling each one three-quarters full. • Bake for 25–30 minutes, until golden brown and firm to the touch. • Transfer the muffin tin to a wire rack. Let cool completely before removing the cupcakes. • Dust with confectioners' sugar.

> *Rhubarb is low in calories and rich in dietary fiber and vitamins C and K, calcium, magnesium, and manganese. Many believe that it helps lower blood pressure and ward off cancer. Never eat the leaves, which are toxic.*

MAKES: 12 PREPARATION: 15–20 MINUTES COOKING: 30–40 MINUTES LEVEL: 1

½ cup (75 g) all-purpose (plain) flour
½ cup (75 g) self-rising flour
½ teaspoon baking soda (bicarbonate of soda)
½ teaspoon ground nutmeg
½ teaspoon cinnamon
⅛ teaspoon salt
⅓ cup (90 g) unsalted butter, softened

½ cup (100 g) firmly packed light brown sugar
2 large eggs
⅓ cup (90 ml) sour cream
2 medium overripe bananas, peeled and mashed, plus ½ banana, thinly sliced

BANANA SOUR CREAM CUPCAKES

Preheat the oven to 325°F (170°C/gas 3).
• Line a standard 12-cup muffin tin with paper liners. • Combine both flours, baking soda, nutmeg, cinnamon, and salt in a small bowl.
• Beat the butter and brown sugar in a medium bowl with an electric mixer on medium-high speed until creamy. • Add the eggs one at a time, beating until just blended after each addition. • With mixer on low speed, add the mixed dry ingredients, alternating with the sour cream. • Stir the mashed banana in by hand.
• Spoon the batter into the prepared cups, filling each one three-quarters full. Top each one with a slice of banana. • Bake for 25–30 minutes, until golden brown and firm to the touch. • Transfer the muffin tin to a wire rack. Let cool completely before removing the cupcakes.

66 *If you don't have self-rising flour on hand, substitute with the same quantity of all-purpose (plain) flour and ¾ teaspoon of baking powder.*

MAKES: 12 PREPARATION: 15 MINUTES COOKING: 25–30 MINUTES LEVEL: 1

1¼	cups (180 g) all-purpose (plain) flour	½	cup (100 g) sugar
2	teaspoons ground cinnamon	2	large eggs
1	teaspoon baking powder	½	cup (125 ml) milk
¼	teaspoon ground cloves	¾	cup (135 g) tart apple, such as Granny Smith or Greening, peeled, cored, and finely chopped
⅛	teaspoon salt	⅓	cup (60 g) raisins
½	cup (125 g) unsalted butter, softened	2	tablespoons Demerara sugar

APPLE & RAISIN CUPCAKES

Preheat the oven to 325°F (170°C/gas 3).
• Line a standard 12-cup muffin tin with paper liners. • Combine the flour, 1 teaspoon of cinnamon, baking powder, cloves, and salt in a small bowl. • Beat the butter and sugar in a medium bowl with an electric mixer on medium-high speed until pale and creamy.
• Add the eggs one at a time, beating until just blended after each addition. • With mixer on low speed, add the mixed dry ingredients, alternating with the milk. • Stir the apple and raisins in by hand. • Spoon the batter into the prepared cups, filling each one three-quarters full. • Combine the remaining cinnamon and Demerara sugar in a small bowl and sprinkle over the cupcakes. • Bake for 25–30 minutes, until golden brown and firm to the touch.
• Transfer the muffin tin to a wire rack. Let cool completely before removing the cupcakes.

66 *Make these healthy muffins in the morning and serve them warm for breakfast.*

MAKES: 12 PREPARATION: 15 MINUTES COOKING: 25–30 MINUTES LEVEL: 1

CUPCAKES

1¼	cups (180 g) all - purpose (plain) flour
1	teaspoon baking powder
⅛	teaspoon salt
½	cup (125 g) unsalted butter, softened
½	cup (100 g) sugar
1	teaspoon finely grated lemon zest
2	large eggs
⅓	cup (90 ml) plain yogurt
1	cup (150 g) fresh or frozen (thawed) blueberries

TOPPING

½	cup (125 ml) plain yogurt
1	tablespoon honey Fresh blueberries, to decorate

BLUEBERRY & YOGURT CUPCAKES

Preheat the oven to 350°F (180°C/gas 4).
• Line a standard 12-cup muffin tin with paper liners. • **Cupcakes:** Combine the flour, baking powder, and salt in a small bowl. • Beat the butter, sugar, and lemon zest in a medium bowl with an electric mixer on medium-high speed until pale and creamy. • Add the eggs one at a time, beating until just blended after each addition. • With mixer on low speed, add the mixed dry ingredients and yogurt. • Stir the blueberries in by hand. • Spoon the batter into the prepared cups, filling each one three-quarters full. • Bake for 20-25 minutes, until golden brown and firm to the touch. • Transfer the muffin tin to a wire rack. Let cool completely before removing the cupcakes.
• **Topping:** Mix the yogurt and honey in a small bowl. • Top each cupcake with a dollop of sweetened yogurt and a few fresh blueberries.

66 *Rich in vitamin C and dietary fiber, blueberries are always a healthy food choice.*

MAKES: 12 PREPARATION: 15 MINUTES COOKING: 20–25 MINUTES LEVEL: 1

1¼ cups (180 g) all-purpose (plain) flour
2 tablespoons ground almonds
1 teaspoon baking powder
⅛ teaspoon salt
½ cup (125 g) unsalted butter, softened

⅓ cup (90 ml) honey
1 teaspoon finely grated lemon zest
2 large eggs
¼ cup (60 ml) milk
½ cup (125 g) fresh or frozen (thawed) blueberries, mashed

BLUEBERRY SWIRL CUPCAKES

Preheat the oven to 325°F (170°C/gas 3). • Line a standard 12-cup muffin tin with paper liners. • Combine the flour, almonds, baking powder, and salt in a small bowl. • Beat the butter, honey, and lemon zest in a medium bowl with an electric mixer on medium-high speed until pale and creamy. • Add the eggs one at a time, beating until just blended after each addition. • With mixer on low speed, add the mixed dry ingredients, alternating with the milk. • Stir the blueberries in by hand to create a swirl pattern. • Spoon the batter into the prepared cups, filling each one three-quarters full. • Bake for 25–30 minutes, until golden brown and firm to the touch. • Transfer the muffin tin to a wire rack. Let cool completely before removing the cupcakes.

" Dress these tasty little cakes up by choosing a pretty decorated paper. Cut into strips to wrap around the cupcakes, cutting the tops with scalloped scissors. After baking, wrap the cupcakes with the paper and hold in place with tape.

MAKES: 12 PREPARATION: 25 MINUTES COOKING: 25–30 MINUTES LEVEL: 1

1	cup (150 g) self-rising flour	¾ cup (150 g) firmly packed light brown sugar
⅓	cup (50 g) all-purpose (plain) flour	1 teaspoon vanilla extract (essence)
⅛	teaspoon salt	2 large eggs
½	cup (125 g) unsalted butter, softened	½ cup (125 ml) milk

½ cup (90 g) dates, coarsely chopped, plus 6 whole dates, halved lengthways

¼ cup (30 g) walnuts, coarsely chopped, plus 12 walnut halves

DATE & WALNUT CUPCAKES

Preheat the oven to 350°F (180°C/gas 4).
• Line a standard 12-cup muffin tin with paper liners. • Combine both flours and the salt in a small bowl. • Beat the butter, brown sugar, and vanilla in a medium bowl with an electric mixer on medium-high speed until creamy. • Add the eggs one at a time, beating until just blended after each addition. • With mixer on low speed, add the mixed dry ingredients, alternating with the milk. • Stir the chopped dates and walnuts in by hand. • Spoon the batter into the prepared cups, filling each one three-quarters full. Top each one with a date and walnut half. • Bake for 20–25 minutes, until golden brown and firm to the touch. • Transfer the muffin tin to a wire rack. Let cool completely before removing the cupcakes.

66 *The dates and walnuts add a pleasant chewy crunch to these cupcakes, as well as a healthy boost of protein, vitamins, minerals, and dietary fiber.*

MAKES: 12 PREPARATION: 15–20 MINUTES COOKING: 20–25 MINUTES LEVEL: 1

½ cup (75 g) whole-wheat (wholemeal) flour	¾ cup (150 g) firmly packed light brown sugar	¼ cup (40 g) pecans, coarsely chopped
1 cup (100 g) ground almonds	2 large eggs	6 canned whole plums in natural syrup, drained, halved, and pitted
1 teaspoon baking powder	1 teaspoon vanilla extract (essence)	
1 teaspoon allspice or pumpkin pie spice	½ cup (125 ml) no-fat milk	

PLUM & PECAN CUPCAKES

Preheat the oven to 325°F (170°C/gas 3). • Line a standard 12-cup muffin tin with paper liners. • Combine the flour, almonds, baking powder, and spice in a small bowl. • Beat the brown sugar, eggs, and vanilla in a medium bowl with an electric mixer on medium-high speed until creamy. • With mixer on low speed, add the mixed dry ingredients alternating with the milk. • Spoon the batter into the prepared cups, filling each one three-quarters full. Place a plum half cut-side down on top of each one. Top each one with a little of the pecans. • Bake for 25–30 minutes, until golden brown and firm to the touch. • Transfer the muffin tin to a wire rack. Let cool completely before removing the cupcakes.

" *Allspice, also known as pimento, is a single spice that tastes like a combination of cinnamon, cloves, ginger, and nutmeg. The best brands are now made in Jamaica.*

MAKES: 12 PREPARATION: 15–20 MINUTES COOKING: 25–30 MINUTES LEVEL: 1

1	cup (150 g) all-purpose (plain) flour	2	teaspoons finely grated orange zest
⅓	cup (30 g) ground almonds	2	large eggs
1	teaspoon baking powder	3	tablespoons fresh or canned passion fruit pulp, strained
⅛	teaspoon salt	2	tablespoons plain yogurt
⅓	cup (90 g) unsalted butter, softened		Confectioners' (icing) sugar, to dust
½	cup (100 g) sugar		

ORANGE PASSION CUPCAKES

Preheat the oven to 350°F (180°C/gas 4). • Line a standard 12-cup muffin tin with paper liners. • Combine the flour, almonds, baking powder, and salt in a small bowl. • Beat the butter, sugar, and orange zest in a medium bowl with an electric mixer on medium-high speed until pale and creamy. • Add the eggs one at a time, beating until just blended after each addition. • With mixer on low speed, add the mixed dry ingredients, passion fruit pulp, and yogurt. • Spoon the batter into the prepared cups, filling each one three-quarters full. • Bake for 20–25 minutes, until golden brown and firm to the touch. • Transfer the muffin tin to a wire rack. Let cool completely before removing the cupcakes. • Dust with confectioners' sugar.

" *Passion fruit have an unmistakable and delectable tropical flavor. They are rich in vitamins A and C as well as dietary fiber.*

MAKES: 12 PREPARATION: 15–20 MINUTES COOKING: 20–25 MINUTES LEVEL: 1

1¼ cups (180 g) all-purpose (plain) flour
1 teaspoon baking powder
⅛ teaspoon salt
½ cup (125 g) unsalted butter, softened
½ cup (100 g) sugar

½ teaspoon vanilla extract (essence)
2 large eggs
⅓ cup (90 ml) milk
⅓ cup (90 g) canned peaches, diced, plus extra, to decorate

¼ cup (60 g) fresh or frozen (thawed) raspberries, plus extra, to decorate

PEACH MELBA CUPCAKES

Preheat the oven to 350°F (180°C/gas 4).
• Line a standard 12-cup muffin tin with paper liners. • Combine the flour, baking powder, and salt in a small bowl. • Beat the butter, sugar, and vanilla in a medium bowl with an electric mixer on medium-high speed until pale and creamy. • Add the eggs one at a time, beating until just blended after each addition. • With mixer on low speed, add the mixed dry ingredients, alternating with the milk. • Stir the diced peaches and raspberries in by hand. • Spoon the batter into the prepared cups, filling each one three-quarters full. Top each one with a peach slice and a raspberry. • Bake for 20–25 minutes, until golden brown and firm to the touch. • Transfer the muffin tin to a wire rack. Let cool completely before removing the cupcakes.

66 *These cupcakes are inspired by the famous dessert created in 1893 by the great French chef Auguste Escoffier at the Savoy Hotel in London, in honor of the Australian soprano Dame Nellie Melba.*

MAKES: 12 PREPARATION: 20 MINUTES COOKING: 20–25 MINUTES LEVEL: 1

1	cup (150 g) self-rising flour	⅛	teaspoon salt	2	tablespoons milk
⅓	cup (50 g) all-purpose (plain) flour	½	cup (125 g) unsalted butter, softened	2	tablespoons freshly squeezed lemon juice, strained
⅓	cup (30 g) ground almonds	¾	cup (150 g) sugar		
¼	cup (30 g) poppy seeds	2	teaspoons finely grated lemon zest		
		2	large eggs		

LEMON & POPPY SEED CUPCAKES

Preheat the oven to 350°F (180°C/gas 4). • Line a standard 12-cup muffin tin with paper liners. • Combine both flours, almonds, poppy seeds, and salt in a small bowl. • Beat the butter, sugar, and lemon zest in a medium bowl with an electric mixer on medium-high speed until pale and creamy. • Add the eggs one at a time, beating until just blended after each addition. • With mixer on low speed, add the mixed dry ingredients, alternating with the milk and lemon juice. • Spoon the batter into the prepared cups, filling each one three-quarters full. • Bake for 20–25 minutes, until golden brown and firm to the touch. • Transfer the muffin tin to a wire rack. Let cool completely before removing the cupcakes.

66 *If you don't have self-rising flour on hand, substitute with the same quantity of all-purpose (plain) flour and 1 teaspoon of baking powder.*

MAKES: 12 PREPARATION: 15 MINUTES COOKING: 20–25 MINUTES LEVEL: 1

1	(14-ounce/400-g) can pear halves, in natural syrup	1	teaspoon baking soda (bicarbonate of soda)	¾	cup (150 g) firmly packed light brown sugar
1	cup (100 g) rolled oats	½	teaspoon baking powder	1	teaspoon vanilla extract (essence)
1	cup (150 g) all-purpose (plain) flour	2	teaspoons ground ginger	2	large eggs
1	cup (150 g) whole-wheat (wholemeal) flour	½	cup (125 g) low-fat dairy-free spread	2	tablespoons flaked almonds

PEAR & OAT CUPCAKES

Preheat the oven to 325°F (170°C/gas 3).
• Line two standard 12-cup muffin tins with 16 paper liners. • Drain the pear syrup into a small saucepan. Add the oats to the syrup and bring to the simmer over medium-high heat. Remove from the heat and set aside for 15 minutes.
• Thinly slice 2–3 pear halves for decoration. (The remaining pears can be served with the cupcakes.) • Combine both flours, baking soda, baking powder, and ginger in a small bowl.
• Beat the low fat spread, brown sugar, and vanilla in a medium bowl with an electric mixer on medium-high speed until pale and creamy.
• Add the eggs one at a time, beating until just blended after each addition. • With mixer on low speed, add the mixed dry ingredients and oat mixture. • Spoon the batter into the prepared cups, filling each one three-quarters full. Arrange the thinly sliced pears decoratively on top and sprinkle with the flaked almonds.
• Bake for 25–30 minutes, until golden brown and firm to the touch. • Transfer the muffin tins to a wire rack. Let cool completely before removing the cupcakes.

66 These cupcakes are pretty and delicious. You can serve them safely and happily to a group that includes diabetics. Everyone will love them!

MAKES: 16   PREPARATION: 20 MINUTES + 15 MINUTES TO REST   COOKING: 25–30 MINUTES   LEVEL: 1

1¼ cups (180 g) all-purpose (plain) flour
1 teaspoon baking powder
½ teaspoon, ground ginger
⅛ teaspoon salt
½ cup (125 g) unsalted butter, softened

½ cup (100 g) firmly packed dark brown sugar
1 tablespoon corn (golden) syrup
2 large eggs
½ cup (125 ml) milk

¾ cup (135 g) ripe pear, cored and finely chopped, plus extra, thinly sliced, to decorate
2 tablespoons candied (glacé) ginger, finely chopped

PEAR & GINGER CUPCAKES

Preheat the oven to 325°F (170°C/gas 3).
• Line a standard 12-cup muffin tin with paper liners. • Combine the flour, baking powder, ginger, and salt in a small bowl. • Beat the butter, brown sugar, and corn syrup in a medium bowl with an electric mixer on medium-high speed, until creamy. • Add the eggs one at a time, beating until just blended after each addition. • With mixer on low speed, add the mixed dry ingredients, alternating with the milk. • Stir the chopped pear and ginger in by hand. • Spoon the batter into the prepared cups, filling each one three-quarters full. Top each one with pear slices. • Bake for 25–30 minutes, until golden brown and firm to the touch. • Transfer the muffin tin to a wire rack. Let cool completely before removing the cupcakes.

" *If you like candied (glacé) ginger, add a few pieces to the top of each cupcake along with the pears.*

MAKES: 12 PREPARATION: 20 MINUTES COOKING: 25–30 MINUTES LEVEL: 1

1   cup (150 g) self-rising flour
⅓   cup (50 g) all-purpose (plain) flour
⅛   teaspoon salt
⅓   cup (30 g) ground almonds
½   cup (125 g) unsalted butter, softened

⅔   cup (150 g) firmly packed light brown sugar
½   teaspoon vanilla extract (essence)
2   large eggs
½   cup (125 ml) milk

½   cup (90 g) dried apricots, thinly sliced, plus extra, to decorate
¼   cup (25 g) flaked almonds, plus extra, to decorate

APRICOT & ALMOND CUPCAKES

Preheat the oven to 350°F (180°C/gas 4).
• Line a standard 12-cup muffin tin with paper liners. • Combine both flours, almonds, and salt in a small bowl. • Beat the butter, brown sugar, and vanilla in a medium bowl with an electric mixer on medium-high speed until creamy.
• Add the eggs one at a time, beating until just blended after each addition. • With mixer on low speed, add the mixed dry ingredients, alternating with the milk. • Stir the apricots and flaked almonds in by hand. • Spoon the batter into the prepared cups, filling each one three-quarters full. • Decorate the tops with pieces of apricot and flaked almonds. • Bake for 20–25 minutes, until golden brown and firm to the touch. • Transfer the muffin tin to a wire rack. Let cool completely before removing the cupcakes.

❝ If you don't have self-rising flour on hand, substitute with the same quantity of all-purpose (plain) flour and 1 teaspoon of baking powder.

MAKES: 12 PREPARATION: 20 MINUTES COOKING: 20–25 MINUTES LEVEL: 1

½ cup (75 g) all-purpose (plain) flour
½ cup (75 g) whole-wheat (wholemeal) flour
1 teaspoon ground cinnamon

1½ teaspoons baking powder
½ cup (125 g) low-fat dairy-free spread
½ cup (100 g) firmly packed light brown sugar

1 teaspoon vanilla extract (essence)
3 large eggs, separated
16 canned apricot halves, in natural syrup, drained

APRICOT CUPCAKES

Preheat the oven to 325°F (170°C/gas 3). • Line two standard 12-cup muffin tins with 16 paper liners. • Combine both flours, cinnamon, and baking powder in a small bowl. • Beat the low fat spread, brown sugar, and vanilla in a medium bowl with an electric mixer on medium-high speed until creamy. • Add the egg yolks one at a time, beating until just blended after each addition. • With mixer on low speed, add the mixed dry ingredients.

• Whisk the egg whites in a small bowl using an electric mixer until soft peaks form. Fold the whites into the batter. • Spoon the batter into the prepared cups, filling each one three-quarters full. • Place apricot halves, cut-side down, on top of each one. • Bake for 25–30 minutes, until golden brown and firm to the touch. • Transfer the muffin tins to a wire rack. Let cool completely before removing the cupcakes.

66 *Apricots are a good source of beta-carotene (which is made into vitamin A in the body). The canning process does not destroy the beta-carotene.*

MAKES: 16 PREPARATION: 15 MINUTES COOKING: 25–30 MINUTES LEVEL: 1

1	cup (150 g) all-purpose (plain) flour	
¼	cup (30 g) shredded (desiccated) coconut	
1	teaspoon baking powder	
⅛	teaspoon salt	

⅓	cup (90 g) unsalted butter, softened
½	cup (100 g) sugar
1	teaspoon finely grated lemon zest
2	large eggs

¼	cup (60 ml) fresh or canned passion fruit pulp, strained
⅓	cup (90 ml) fresh or canned passion fruit pulp, to drizzle

44

PASSION FRUIT CUPCAKES

Preheat the oven to 350°F (180°C/gas 4). • Line a standard 12-cup muffin tin with paper liners. • Combine the flour, coconut, baking powder, and salt in a small bowl. • Beat the butter, sugar, and lemon zest in a medium bowl with an electric mixer on medium-high speed until pale and creamy. • Add the eggs one at a time, beating until just blended after each addition. • With mixer on low speed, add the mixed dry ingredients and strained passion fruit pulp. • Spoon the batter into the prepared cups, filling each one three-quarters full. • Bake for 20–25 minutes, until golden brown and firm to the touch. • Transfer the muffin tin to a wire rack. Let cool completely before removing the cupcakes. • Drizzle with the unstrained passion fruit pulp.

66 *Serve these pretty cupcakes with tea or coffee at snack time or to finish a family lunch or dinner.*

MAKES: 12 PREPARATION: 15–20 MINUTES COOKING: 20–25 MINUTES LEVEL: 1

1	cup (150 g) all-purpose (plain) flour	⅓	cup (90 g) unsalted butter, softened	3	tablespoons freshly squeezed orange juice, strained
⅓	cup (30 g) ground almonds	½	cup (100 g) sugar	2	tablespoons plain yogurt
1	teaspoon baking powder	2	teaspoons finely grated orange zest	⅓	cup (100 g) orange marmalade
¼	teaspoon ground ginger	5	cardamom pods, seeds removed and crushed		
⅛	teaspoon salt	2	large eggs		

CARDAMOM & ORANGE CUPCAKES

Preheat the oven to 350°F (180°C/gas 4).
• Line a standard 12-cup muffin tin with paper liners. • Combine the flour, almonds, baking powder, ginger, and salt in a small bowl. • Beat the butter, sugar, orange zest, and crushed cardamom seeds in a medium bowl with an electric mixer on medium-high speed until pale and creamy. • Add the eggs one at a time, beating until just blended after each addition.

• With mixer on low speed, add the mixed dry ingredients, alternating with the orange juice and yogurt. • Spoon the batter into the prepared cups, filling each one three-quarters full. • Bake for 20–25 minutes, until golden brown and firm to the touch. • Transfer the muffin tin to a wire rack. Let cool completely before removing the cupcakes. • Spread each cupcake with a little orange marmalade.

66 *Cardamom has a strong, unique taste, with an intensely aromatic fragrance. Be sure to buy the pods and crush just before use; the flavor is so much better.*

MAKES: 12 PREPARATION: 20 MINUTES COOKING: 20–25 MINUTES LEVEL: 1

CUPCAKES

1⅓ cups (200 g) all-purpose (plain) flour

1½ teaspoons baking powder

½ teaspoon ground cinnamon

½ teaspoon ground nutmeg

⅛ teaspoon salt

⅔ cup (150 ml) sunflower oil

½ cup (100 g) firmly packed light brown sugar

2 large eggs, lightly beaten

2 medium carrots (150 g), grated

⅓ cup (50 g) walnuts, coarsely chopped

FROSTING

½ cup (125 ml) mascarpone cheese

1 tablespoon honey Coarsely chopped walnuts, to decorate

CARROT & WALNUT CUPCAKES

Preheat the oven to 350°F (180°C/gas 4). • Line a standard 12-cup muffin tin with paper liners. • **Cupcakes:** Combine the flour, baking powder, cinnamon, nutmeg, and salt in a small bowl. • Combine the oil, sugar, and eggs in a medium bowl. Stir in the carrots and walnuts. Mix in the dry ingredients until well combined. • Spoon the batter into the prepared cups, filling each one three-quarters full. • Bake for 20–25 minutes, until golden brown and firm to the touch. • Transfer the muffin tin to a wire rack. Let cool completely before removing the cupcakes. • **Frosting:** Mix the mascarpone cheese and honey in a small bowl. • Top each cupcake with a dollop of sweetened mascarpone and few chopped walnut pieces.

❝ For a slightly different flavor, substitute the walnuts with the same quantity of pecans.

MAKES: 12 PREPARATION: 15 MINUTES COOKING: 20–25 MINUTES LEVEL: 1

1	cup (150 g) self-rising flour	½	cup (125 g) unsalted butter, softened	2	tablespoons freshly squeezed lemon juice, strained
⅓	cup (50 g) all-purpose (plain) flour	½	cup (100 g) sugar	1	tablespoon milk
¼	cup (40 g) fine-ground yellow cornmeal	2	teaspoons finely grated lemon zest		Confectioners' (icing sugar, to dust
⅛	teaspoon salt	2	large eggs		
		⅓	cup (90 ml) sour cream		

LEMON SOUR CUPCAKES

Preheat the oven to 350°F (180°C/gas 4).
• Line a standard 12-cup muffin tin with paper liners. • Combine both flours, cornmeal, and salt in a small bowl. • Beat the butter, sugar, and lemon zest in a medium bowl with an electric mixer on medium-high speed until pale and creamy. • Add the eggs one at a time, beating until just blended after each addition. • With mixer on low speed, add the mixed dry ingredients, alternating with the sour cream, lemon juice, and milk. • Spoon the batter into the prepared cups, filling each one three-quarters full. • Bake for 20–25 minutes, until golden brown and firm to the touch. • Transfer the muffin tin to a wire rack. Let cool completely before removing the cupcakes. • Dust with confectioners' sugar.

❝ *If you don't have self-rising flour on hand, substitute with the same quantity of all-purpose (plain) flour and 1 teaspoon of baking powder.*

MAKES: 12 PREPARATION: 20 MINUTES COOKING: 20–25 MINUTES LEVEL: 1

1¼ cups (180 g) all-purpose (plain) flour	½ cup (125 g) unsalted butter, softened	½ cup (125 ml) milk
1 teaspoon baking powder	⅓ cup (70 g) sugar	⅓ cup (60 g) dried cranberries
½ teaspoon ground cinnamon	3 tablespoons maple syrup, plus extra, to glaze	¼ cup (30 g) walnuts, coarsely chopped
⅛ teaspoon salt	2 large eggs	

CRANBERRY & WALNUT CUPCAKES

Preheat the oven to 350°F (180°C/gas 4).
• Line a standard 12-cup muffin tin with paper liners. • Combine the flour, baking powder, cinnamon, and salt in a small bowl. • Beat the butter, sugar, and maple syrup in a medium bowl with an electric mixer on medium-high speed until pale and creamy. • Add the eggs one at a time, beating until just blended after each addition. • With mixer on low speed, add the mixed dry ingredients, alternating with the milk. • Stir the cranberries and walnuts in by hand. • Spoon the batter into the prepared cups, filling each one three-quarters full. • Bake for 20–25 minutes, until golden brown and firm to the touch. • Brush the tops with extra maple syrup while the cupcakes are still hot. • Transfer the muffin tin to a wire rack. Let cool completely before removing the cupcakes.

" These cupcakes are delicious year round, but you may like to serve them for breakfast at Thanksgiving.

MAKES: 12 PREPARATION: 15 MINUTES COOKING: 20–25 MINUTES LEVEL: 1

CUPCAKES

1½ cups (225 g) all-purpose (plain) flour
1½ teaspoons baking powder
1 tablespoon chai tea powder
⅛ teaspoon salt
½ cup (125 g) unsalted butter, softened

½ cup (100 g) firmly packed light brown sugar
1 teaspoon vanilla extract (essence)
2 large eggs
½ cup (125 ml) milk

TOPPING

½ cup (125 ml) heavy (double) cream
1 teaspoon ground cinnamon

54

CHAI CUPCAKES

Preheat the oven to 350°F (180°C/gas 4).
• Line a standard 12-cup muffin tin with paper liners. • **Cupcakes:** Combine the flour, baking powder, chai powder, and salt in a small bowl. • Beat the butter, brown sugar, and vanilla in a medium bowl with an electric mixer on medium-high speed until creamy. • Add the eggs one at a time, beating until just blended after each addition. • With mixer on low speed, add the mixed dry ingredients, alternating with the milk. • Spoon the batter into the prepared cups, filling each one three-quarters full. • Bake for 20–25 minutes, until golden brown and firm to the touch. • Transfer the muffin tin to a wire rack. Let cool completely before removing the cupcakes. • **Topping:** Beat the cream until thickened. Spoon a little on top of each cupcake and dust with the cinnamon.

66 *The word "chai" comes from China, the home of tea (where tea is known as chà). Chai powder is available in gourmet food stores and from online suppliers.*

MAKES: 12 PREPARATION: 20 MINUTES COOKING: 20–25 MINUTES LEVEL: 1

1⅓ cups (150 g) all-purpose (plain) flour	⅔ cup (150 g) sugar	½ cup (90 g) pitted prunes, coarsely chopped
⅓ cup (30 g) ground almonds	½ teaspoon vanilla extract (essence)	¼ cup (25 g) slivered almonds
1½ teaspoons baking powder	1 teaspoon finely grated orange zest	Confectioners' (icing) sugar, to dust
⅛ teaspoon salt	2 large eggs	
½ cup (125 g) unsalted butter, softened	½ cup (125 ml) butter milk	

PRUNE & ALMOND CUPCAKES

Preheat the oven to 350°F (180°C/gas 4).
• Line a standard 12-cup muffin tin with paper liners. • Combine the flour, almonds, baking powder, and salt in a small bowl. • Beat the butter, sugar, vanilla, and orange zest in a medium bowl with an electric mixer on medium-high speed until pale and creamy.
• Add the eggs one at a time, beating until just blended after each addition. • With mixer on low speed, add the mixed dry ingredients, alternating with the butter milk. • Stir the prunes and almonds in by hand. • Spoon the batter into the prepared cups, filling each one three-quarters full. • Bake for 20–25 minutes, until golden brown and firm to the touch.
• Transfer the muffin tin to a wire rack. Let cool completely before removing the cupcakes.
• Dust with confectioners' sugar.

" Prunes are packed with energy and dietary fiber, making these cupcakes perfect for breakfast or brunch.

MAKES: 12 PREPARATION: 20 MINUTES COOKING: 20–25 MINUTES LEVEL: 1

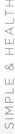

1⅓	cup (200 g) all-purpose (plain) flour	½	cup (100 g) sugar	¾	cup (150 g) canned crushed pineapple, drained
⅔	cup (80 g) shredded (desiccated) coconut	1	teaspoon finely grated lemon zest	½	cup (100 g) pineapple pieces, drained
1	teaspoon baking powder	2	large eggs		
⅛	teaspoon salt	3	tablespoons plain yogurt		
½	cup (125 g) unsalted butter, softened	2	tablespoons pineapple juice		

PINEAPPLE CUPCAKES

Preheat the oven to 325°F (170°C/gas 3). • Line a standard 12-cup muffin tin with paper liners. • Combine the flour, half the coconut, baking powder, and salt in a small bowl. • Beat the butter, sugar, and lemon zest in a medium bowl with an electric mixer on medium-high speed until pale and creamy. • Add the eggs one at a time, beating until just blended after each addition. • With mixer on low speed, add the mixed dry ingredients, alternating with the yogurt and pineapple juice. • Stir the crushed pineapple in by hand. • Spoon the batter into the prepared cups, filling each one three-quarters full. Top each one with pineapple pieces and sprinkle with the remaining coconut. • Bake for 25–30 minutes, until golden brown and firm to the touch. • Transfer the muffin tin to a wire rack. Let cool completely before removing the cupcakes.

66 *Pineapple is healthy and nutritious. It has no cholesterol and very little fat and sodium, yet is packed with vitamin C and dietary fiber.*

MAKES: 12 PREPARATION: 20 MINUTES COOKING: 25–30 MINUTES LEVEL: 1

1	cup (150 g) all-purpose (plain) flour	½	cup (125 g) unsalted butter, softened	½	cup (125 g) canned plums, pitted and chopped, plus extra, sliced, to decorate
⅓	cup (30 g) ground hazelnuts	½	cup (100 g) firmly packed light brown sugar		
1	teaspoon baking powder	2	large eggs	¼	cup (40 g) hazelnuts, coarsely chopped
1	teaspoon ground cinnamon	½	cup (125 ml) milk		
⅛	teaspoon salt				

PLUM & HAZELNUT CUPCAKES

Preheat the oven to 325°F (170°C/gas 3).
• Line a standard 12-cup muffin tin with paper liners. • Combine the flour, ground hazelnuts, baking powder, cinnamon, and salt in a small bowl. • Beat the butter and brown sugar in a medium bowl with an electric mixer on medium-high speed until creamy. • Add the eggs one at a time, beating until just blended after each addition. • With mixer on low speed, add the mixed dry ingredients, alternating with the milk. • Stir the chopped plums and hazelnuts in by hand. • Spoon the batter into the prepared cups, filling each one three-quarters full. Top each one with plum slices. • Bake for 25–30 minutes, until golden brown and firm to the touch. • Transfer the muffin tin to a wire rack. Let cool completely before removing the cupcakes.

66 *In late summer and early fall, when plums are in season, use very ripe fresh plums to make these cupcakes.*

MAKES: 12 PREPARATION: 15 MINUTES COOKING: 25–30 MINUTES LEVEL: 1

¾	cup (125 g) all-purpose (plain) flour	½	cup (100 g) sugar	½ cup (125 g) fresh or canned mango cheeks, coarsely chopped, plus extra, to decorate
½	cup (60 g) shredded (desiccated) coconut	2	teaspoons finely grated lime zest	
1	teaspoon baking powder	2	large eggs	
⅛	teaspoon salt	¼	cup (60 ml) coconut milk	Coconut flakes, to decorate
½	cup (125 g) unsalted butter, softened	½	tablespoon freshly squeezed lime juice	

MANGO & COCONUT CUPCAKES

Preheat the oven to 325°F (170°C/gas 3).
• Line a standard 12-cup muffin tin with paper liners. • Combine the flour, shredded coconut, baking powder, and salt in a small bowl. • Beat the butter, sugar, and lime zest in a medium bowl with an electric mixer on medium-high speed until pale and creamy. • Add the eggs one at a time, beating until just blended after each addition. • With mixer on low speed, add the mixed dry ingredients, alternating with the coconut milk and lime juice. • Stir the mango in by hand. • Spoon the batter into the prepared cups, filling each one three-quarters full. • Bake for 25–30 minutes, until golden brown and firm to the touch. • Transfer the muffin tin to a wire rack. Let cool completely before removing the cupcakes. • Top each one with mango slices and coconut flakes.

Sweet, flavorful mangoes originally came from India. This exotic fruit is easy to digest and packed with vitamins and minerals.

MAKES: 12 PREPARATION: 15–20 MINUTES COOKING: 25–30 MINUTES LEVEL: 1

DIABETICS FRIENDLY

1¼	cups (180 g) whole-wheat (wholemeal) flour	½	cup (125 g) low-fat dairy-free spread	1	cup (250 ml) low fat plain yogurt, plus extra, to decorate
1	teaspoon baking powder	¾	cup (150 g) firmly packed light brown sugar	2	medium overripe bananas, mashed
½	teaspoon baking soda (bicarbonate of soda)	1	teaspoon vanilla extract (essence)		
1	teaspoon ground nutmeg, plus extra, to dust	2	large eggs		

BANANA & YOGURT CUPCAKES

Preheat the oven to 350°F (180°C/gas 4).
• Line a standard 12-cup muffin tin with paper liners. • Combine the flour, baking powder, baking soda, and nutmeg in a small bowl.
• Beat the low-fat spread, brown sugar, and vanilla in a medium bowl with an electric mixer on medium-high speed until creamy. • Add the eggs one at a time, beating until just blended after each addition. • With mixer on low speed, add the mixed dry ingredients, alternating with half of the yogurt. • Stir the banana in by hand.
• Spoon the batter into the prepared cups, filling each one three-quarters full. • Bake for 20–25 minutes, until golden brown and firm to the touch. • Transfer the muffin tin to a wire rack. Let cool completely before removing the cupcakes. • Place a dollop of the remaining yogurt on top of each one and dust with nutmeg.

" *Serve these exquisite cupcakes to the whole family at breakfast.*

MAKES: 12 PREPARATION: 15–20 MINUTES COOKING: 20–25 MINUTES LEVEL: 1

1¼	cups (180 g) all-purpose (plain) flour	1	teaspoon vanilla extract (essence)	2	tablespoons finely chopped fresh mint leaves, plus 1 tablespoon extra, to decorate
1	teaspoon baking powder	2	large eggs		
½	teaspoon ground cinnamon	⅓	cup (90 ml) single (light) cream	1	tablespoon vanilla sugar
⅛	teaspoon salt	1	cup (150 g) fresh strawberries, coarsely chopped, plus 3–4 extra, sliced, to decorate	⅓	cup (90 ml) crème fraîche or sour cream
½	cup (125 g) unsalted butter, softened				
½	cup (100 g) sugar				

MINTED STRAWBERRY CUPCAKES

Preheat the oven to 350°F (180°C/gas 4). • Line a standard 12-cup muffin tin with paper liners. • Combine the flour, baking powder, cinnamon, and salt in a small bowl. • Beat the butter, sugar, and vanilla in a medium bowl with an electric mixer on medium-high speed until pale and creamy. • Add the eggs in one at a time, beating until just blended after each addition. • With mixer on low speed, add the mixed dry ingredients, alternating with the cream. • Stir the strawberries and mint in by hand. • Spoon the batter into the prepared cups, filling each one three-quarters full. • Bake for 20–25 minutes, until golden brown and firm to the touch. • Transfer the muffin tin to a wire rack. Let cool completely before removing the cupcakes. • Combine the remaining strawberries, mint, and vanilla sugar in a small bowl. Spoon crème fraîche over the cupcakes and arrange the strawberry mixture on top.

❝ *If you don't have fresh strawberries on hand, replace with the same quantity of fresh raspberries. Replace the vanilla sugar with confectioners' (icing) sugar, if preferred.*

MAKES: 12 PREPARATION: 15–20 MINUTES COOKING: 20–25 MINUTES LEVEL: 1

1⅓ cups (200 g) all-purpose (plain) flour
1 teaspoon baking powder
⅛ teaspoon salt
½ cup (125 g) unsalted butter, softened

⅓ cup (70 g) firmly packed light brown sugar
3 tablespoons honey, plus extra, warmed, to glaze
2 large eggs

½ cup (125 ml) milk
½ cup (90 g) dried figs, sliced, plus extra, to decorate

FIG & HONEY CUPCAKES

Preheat the oven to 350°F (180°C/gas 4). • Line a standard 12-cup muffin tin with paper liners. • Combine the flour, baking powder, and salt in a small bowl. • Beat the butter, brown sugar, and honey in a medium bowl with an electric mixer on medium-high speed until pale and creamy. • Add the eggs one at a time, beating until just blended after each addition. • With mixer on low speed, add the mixed dry ingredients, alternating with the milk. • Stir the figs in by hand. • Spoon the batter into the prepared cups, filling each one three-quarters full. Top each one with a few slices of fig. • Bake for 20–25 minutes, until golden brown and firm to the touch. Brush with the extra honey while the cupcakes are still hot. • Transfer the muffin tin to a wire rack. Let cool completely before removing the cupcakes.

❝ *The fig and honey topping on these cupcakes is scrumptious, as well as healthy and energy-giving. These cupcakes are great for breakfast or can be tucked into a lunch box.*

MAKES: 12 PREPARATION: 15 MINUTES COOKING: 20–25 MINUTES LEVEL: 1

CUPCAKES
- ¾ cup (125 g) all-purpose (plain) flour
- ½ cup (60 g) ground almonds
- 1 teaspoon baking powder
- ⅛ teaspoon salt
- ⅓ cup (90 g) unsalted butter, softened
- ½ cup (100 g) sugar
- 1 teaspoon vanilla extract (essence)
- 1 teaspoon finely grated lemon zest
- 2 large eggs
- ⅓ cup (90 ml) sour cream
- ½ cup (125 g) fresh or frozen (thawed) blackberries

TOPPING
- ½ cup (125 ml) sour cream
- 12 fresh blackberries, to decorate

BLACKBERRY & SOUR CREAM CUPCAKE

Preheat the oven to 325°F (170°C/gas 3).
• Line a standard 12-cup muffin tin with paper liners. • **Cupcakes:** Combine the flour, almonds, baking powder, and salt in a small bowl. • Beat the butter, sugar, vanilla, and lemon zest in a medium bowl with an electric mixer on medium-high speed until pale and creamy.
• Add the eggs one at a time, beating until just blended after each addition. • With mixer on low speed, add the mixed dry ingredients, alternating with the sour cream. • Stir the blackberries in by hand. • Spoon the batter into the prepared cups, filling each one three-quarters full. • Bake for 25–30 minutes, until golden brown and firm to the touch. • Transfer the muffin tin to a wire rack. Let cool completely before removing the cupcakes.
• **Topping:** Top each cupcake with a dollop of the sour cream and a blackberry.

    Blackberries are a good source of vitamins C and K, dietary fiber, and manganese.

MAKES: 12   PREPARATION: 15–20 MINUTES   COOKING: 25–30 MINUTES   LEVEL: 1

⅔ cup (100 g) all-
   purpose (plain) flour
⅓ cup (50 g) self-rising
   flour
½ teaspoon ground
   cinnamon
½ teaspoon ground
   nutmeg
¼ teaspoon ground
   cloves

⅛ teaspoon salt
½ cup (125 g) unsalted
   butter, softened
⅔ cup (150 g) firmly
   packed light brown
   sugar
2 large eggs
¼ cup (60 ml) milk
½ cup (90 g) currants

¼ cup (40 g) slivered
   almonds
¼ cup (25 g) mixed peel
   finely chopped
2–3 tablespoons apricot
   preserves (jam),
   warmed

CURRANT & MIXED PEEL CUPCAKES

Preheat the oven to 325°F (170°C/gas 3).
• Line a standard 12-cup muffin tin with paper
liners. • Combine both flours, cinnamon,
nutmeg, cloves, and salt in a small bowl. • Beat
the butter and brown sugar in a medium bowl
with an electric mixer on medium-high speed
until creamy. • Add the eggs one at a time,
beating until just blended after each addition.
• With mixer on low speed, add the mixed dry
ingredients, alternating with the milk. • Stir the
currants, almonds, and mixed peel in by hand.
• Spoon the batter into the prepared cups,
filling each one three-quarters full. • Bake for
25–30 minutes, until golden brown and firm to
the touch. Brush the cupcakes with the apricot
preserves while still hot. • Transfer the muffin
tin to a wire rack. Let cool completely before
removing the cupcakes.

❝ *These cupcakes are full of energy-
giving dried fruit. Pack them in lunch boxes
or serve warm as an after-school treat.*

MAKES: 12 PREPARATION: 15 MINUTES COOKING: 25–30 MINUTES LEVEL: 1

1½ cups (225 g) all-purpose (plain) flour
¾ cup (150 g) sugar
2 teaspoons allspice or pumpkin spice mix
1½ teaspoons baking powder
1 teaspoon baking soda (bicarbonate of soda)
⅛ teaspoon salt

1 cup (250 ml) milk
½ cup (125 g) unsalted butter, melted
¾ cup (135 g) approximately 1 tart apple, such as Granny Smith or Greening, peeled, cored, and finely chopped
¼ cup (45 g) currants

¼ cup (45 g) raisins
Confectioners' (icing) sugar, to dust

GRANNY'S APPLE CUPCAKES

Preheat the oven to 350°F (180°C/gas 4).
• Line a standard 12-cup muffin tin with paper liners. • Combine the flour, sugar, spice, baking powder, baking soda, and salt in a medium bowl. • Combine the milk and butter in a small bowl. • Pour the milk mixture into the mixed dry ingredients and stir until combined. • Stir the apple, currants and raisins in by hand.
• Spoon the batter into the prepared cups, filling each one three-quarters full. • Bake for 20–25 minutes, until golden brown and firm to the touch. • Transfer the muffin tin to a wire rack. Let cool completely before removing the cupcakes. • Dust with confectioners' sugar.

   These old-fashioned cupcakes will be a hit with the whole family. They do not contain eggs for those who are allergic to them.

MAKES: 12 PREPARATION: 15 MINUTES COOKING: 25–30 MINUTES LEVEL: 1

1 cup (150 g) all-purpose (plain) flour
⅓ cup (30 g) ground hazelnuts
1 teaspoon baking powder
⅛ teaspoon salt
½ cup (125 g) unsalted butter, softened

½ cup (100 g) firmly packed light brown sugar
3 teaspoons freeze-dried coffee granules, dissolved in 1 tablespoon boiling water
2 large eggs

½ cup (125 ml) single (light) cream
½ cup (125 ml) crème fraîche
Chocolate-coated coffee beans, to decorate

FRAPPÈ CUPCAKES

Preheat the oven to 325°F (170°C/gas 3).
• Line a standard 12-cup muffin tin with paper liners. • Combine the flour, hazelnuts, baking powder, and salt in a small bowl. • Beat the butter, brown sugar, and coffee mixture in a medium bowl with an electric mixer on medium-high speed until creamy. • Add the eggs one at a time, beating until just blended after each addition. • With mixer on low speed, add the mixed dry ingredients, alternating with the cream. • Spoon the batter into the prepared cups, filling each one three-quarters full. • Bake for 25–30 minutes, until golden brown and firm to the touch. • Transfer the muffin tin to a wire rack. Let cool completely before removing the cupcakes. • Top each cupcake with a dollop of crème fraîche and finish with 2–3 chocolate-coated coffee beans.

❝ With coffee, nuts, and chocolate, these cupcakes are perfect for a special brunch or coffee morning.

MAKES: 12 PREPARATION: 15–20 MINUTES COOKING: 25–30 MINUTES LEVEL: 1

⅔ cup (100 g) rye flour	¼ cup (50 g) sugar	1 tablespoon candied (glacé) ginger, chopped, plus extra, to decorate
⅓ cup (50 g) rice flour	1 teaspoon vanilla extract (essence)	
3 tablespoons potato flour	3 large eggs	3 tablespoons orange marmalade, warmed and strained, to glaze
½ teaspoon baking powder	½ cup (90 g) dried apricots, coarsely chopped	
¼ teaspoon baking soda (bicarbonate of soda)	2 tablespoons candied (glacé) cherries	
⅛ teaspoon salt		
½ cup (125 g) dairy-free spread		

APRICOT & GINGER CUPCAKES

Preheat the oven to 350°F (180°C/gas 4). • Line a standard 12-cup muffin tin with paper liners. • Sift the flours, baking powder, baking soda, and salt into a medium bowl. • Beat the dairy-free spread, sugar, and vanilla in a medium bowl with an electric mixer on medium-high speed until creamy. • Add the eggs one at a time, beating until just blended after each addition. • With mixer on low speed, add the mixed dry ingredients. • Stir the apricots, cherries, and ginger in by hand. • Spoon the batter into the prepared cups, filling each one three-quarters full. • Bake for 20–25 minutes, until golden brown and firm to the touch. • Transfer the muffin tin to a wire rack. Glaze with orange marmalade. Let cool completely before removing the cupcakes. • Top with candied ginger.

" *When preparing food for those with gluten intolerance always make sure that gluten is not hidden in the baking powder, vanilla extract, or other ingredients. Read labels carefully.*

MAKES: 12   PREPARATION: 15–20 MINUTES   COOKING: 20–25 MINUTES   LEVEL: 1

chocolate
cupcakes

CUPCAKES

2 cups (300 g) all-purpose (plain) flour
⅓ cup (50 g) unsweetened cocoa powder, sifted
2 teaspoons baking powder
1 teaspoon baking soda (bicarbonate of soda)
1 teaspoon ground cinnamon

⅛ teaspoon salt
½ cup (125 g) unsalted butter, melted
1 cup (250 ml) blue agave
1 cup (250 ml) milk
1½ teaspoons vanilla extract (essence)
1 teaspoon finely grated orange zest

TOPPING

½ cup (125 ml) heavy (double) cream
1 teaspoon blue agave
¼ teaspoon ground cinnamon
1 ounce (30 g) sugar-free chocolate, grated, to decorate

CHOCOLATE CUPCAKES

EGG FREE

SUGAR FREE

Preheat the oven to 350°F (180°C/gas 4). • Line two standard 12-cup muffin tins with 16 paper liners. • **Cupcakes:** Combine the flour, cocoa, baking powder, baking soda, cinnamon, and salt in a medium bowl. • Combine the butter, blue agave, milk, vanilla, and orange zest in a medium bowl. • Pour the butter and milk mixture into the mixed dry ingredients and stir until combined. Do not over mix. • Spoon the batter into the prepared cups, filling each one three-quarters full. • Bake for 15–20 minutes, until risen and firm to the touch. • Transfer the muffin tins to a wire rack. Let cool completely before removing the cupcakes • **Topping:** Whisk the cream in a small bowl using an electric mixer on medium speed until it begins to thicken. • Add the blue agave and cinnamon and whisk until soft peaks form. • Spread the cream over the cupcakes and top with grated chocolate.

66 *Blue agave is a natural sweetener extracted from the core of the blue agave plant. It is available at many natural food stores and from online suppliers.*

MAKES: 16 PREPARATION: 20 MINUTES COOKING: 15–20 MINUTES LEVEL: 1

CUPCAKES

3 ounces (90 g) dark chocolate, coarsely chopped
¼ cup (60 ml) light (single) cream
⅔ cup (160 g) smooth peanut butter
⅔ cup (100 g) all-purpose (plain) flour
½ cup (50 g) ground almonds

3 tablespoons unsweetened cocoa powder, sifted
1 teaspoon baking powder
⅛ teaspoon salt
¼ cup (60 g) unsalted butter, softened
1 cup (200 g) firmly packed light brown sugar
2 large eggs

PEANUT TOFFEE

⅓ cup (70 g) sugar
½ cup (50 g) blanched peanuts, coarsely chopped
3 ounces (90 g) dark chocolate, coarsely chopped

CHOCOLATE PEANUT BUTTER CUPCAKES

Preheat the oven to 350°F (180°C/gas 4).
• Line a standard 12-cup muffin tin with paper liners. • **Cupcakes:** Melt the chocolate, cream, and peanut butter in a double boiler over barely simmering water, stirring until smooth. Remove from the heat and let cool. • Combine the flour, almonds, cocoa, baking powder, and salt in a small bowl. • Beat the butter and brown sugar in a medium bowl with an electric mixer on medium-high speed until creamy. • Add the eggs one at a time, beating until just blended after each addition. • With mixer on low speed, add the mixed dry ingredients and melted chocolate mixture. • Spoon the batter into the prepared cups, filling each one three-quarters full. • Bake for 20–25 minutes, until risen and firm to the touch. • Transfer the muffin tin to a wire rack. Let cool completely before removing the cupcakes. • **Peanut Toffee:** Line a baking sheet with parchment paper.
• Put the sugar in a small pan and heat gently until melted and pale gold, about 5 minutes. Add the peanuts and cook, stirring, for 30 seconds. • Pour onto the prepared baking sheet and leave to harden. • Break into small shards.
• Melt the chocolate in a double boiler over simmering water, stirring until smooth. Remove from the heat and let cool a little.
• Spread some chocolate on top of each cupcake. Place shards of peanut toffee on top.

MAKES: 12 PREPARATION: 30 MINUTES COOKING: 35–40 MINUTES LEVEL: 2

CUPCAKES

3   ounces (90 g) dark chocolate, coarsely chopped
⅓ cup (90 ml) light (single) cream
⅔ cup (100 g) all-purpose (plain) flour
½ cup (60 g) shredded (desiccated) coconut

2   tablespoons unsweetened cocoa powder, sifted
1   teaspoon baking powder
⅛ teaspoon salt
⅓ cup (90 g) unsalted butter, softened
1   cup (200 g) sugar
2   large eggs

CHOCOLATE AND COCONUT GANACHE

4   ounces (120 g) dark chocolate, coarsely chopped
¼ cup (60 ml) light (single) cream
¾ cup (90 g) shaved coconut

CHOCOLATE ROUGH CUPCAKES

Preheat the oven to 325°F (170°C/gas 3). • Line a standard 12-cup muffin tin with paper liners. • **Cupcakes:** Melt the chocolate and cream in a double boiler over barely simmering water, stirring until smooth. Remove from the heat and let cool. • Combine the flour, coconut, cocoa, baking powder, and salt in a small bowl. • Beat the butter and sugar in a medium bowl with an electric mixer on medium-high speed until pale and creamy. • Add the eggs one at a time, beating until just blended after each addition. • With mixer on low speed, add the mixed dry ingredients and melted chocolate. • Spoon the batter into the prepared cups, filling each one three-quarters full. • Bake for 25–30 minutes, until risen and firm to the touch. • Transfer the muffin tin to a wire rack. Let cool completely before removing the cupcakes. • **Chocolate and Coconut Ganache:** Melt the chocolate and cream in a double boiler over bravely simmering water, stirring until smooth. Remove from the heat and let cool. • Stir in the coconut. • Spread over the top of each cupcake.

" A divine combination of chocolate and coconut! Serve these cupcakes after dinner with little cups of espresso coffee.

MAKES: 12 PREPARATION: 30 MINUTES COOKING: 30–35 MINUTES LEVEL: 2

CUPCAKES

3 ounces (90 g) dark chocolate, coarsely chopped

⅓ cup (90 ml) light (single) cream

1 cup (150 g) all-purpose (plain) flour

2 tablespoons unsweetened cocoa powder, sifted

1 teaspoon baking powder

⅛ teaspoon salt

⅓ cup (90 g) unsalted butter, softened

1 cup (200 g) firmly packed light brown sugar

2 large eggs

½ cup (90 g) dark chocolate chips

TOPPING

2 ounces (60 g) dark chocolate, coarsely chopped

2 ounces (60 g) milk chocolate, coarsely chopped

DOUBLE CHOCOLATE CUPCAKES

Preheat the oven to 325°F (170°C/gas 3). • Line a standard 12-cup muffin tin with paper liners. • **Cupcakes:** Melt the chocolate and cream in a double boiler over barely simmering water, stirring until smooth. Remove from the heat and let cool. • Combine the flour, cocoa, baking powder, and salt in a small bowl. • Beat the butter and brown sugar in a medium bowl with an electric mixer on medium-high speed until creamy. • Add the eggs one at a time, beating until just blended after each addition. • With mixer on low speed, add the mixed dry ingredients and melted chocolate. • Stir in the chocolate chips by hand. • Spoon the batter into the prepared cups, filling each one three-quarters full. • Bake for 25–30 minutes, until risen and firm to the touch. • Transfer the muffin tin to a wire rack. Let cool completely before removing the cupcakes. • **Topping:** Melt both chocolates in two separate double boilers over barely simmering water, stirring until smooth. Remove from the heat and let cool. • Drizzle the dark chocolate over the top of the cupcakes in one direction and the milk chocolate in the other, creating a crisscross pattern.

If liked, substitute the milk chocolate for the topping with the same quantity of white chocolate.

CUPCAKES

- 3 ounces (90 g) dark chocolate, coarsely chopped
- ⅓ cup (90 ml) light (single) cream
- ⅔ cup (100 g) all-purpose (plain) flour
- ½ cup (50 g) ground hazelnuts
- 2 tablespoons unsweetened cocoa powder, sifted
- 1 teaspoon baking powder
- ⅛ teaspoon salt

- ⅓ cup (90 g) unsalted butter, softened
- 1 cup (200 g) firmly packed light brown sugar
- 2 large eggs
- 1 tablespoon hazelnut liqueur
- ¼ cup (40 g) hazelnuts, toasted and coarsely chopped

CHOCOLATE HAZELNUT FROSTING

- 3 ounces (90 g) dark chocolate, coarsely chopped
- ½ cup (125 g) chocolate hazelnut spread
- 2 tablespoons coarsely chopped hazelnuts, to decorate

CHOCOLATE HAZELNUT CUPCAKES

Preheat the oven to 325°F (170°C/gas 3). • Line a standard 12-cup muffin tin with paper liners. • **Cupcakes:** Melt the chocolate and cream in a double boiler over barely simmering water, stirring until smooth. Remove from the heat and let cool. • Combine the flour, ground hazelnuts, cocoa, baking powder, and salt in a small bowl. • Beat the butter and sugar in a medium bowl with an electric mixer on medium-high speed until creamy. • Add the eggs in one at a time, beating until just blended after each addition. • With mixer on low speed, add the mixed dry ingredients and melted chocolate. • Stir in the hazelnut liqueur and toasted hazelnuts by hand. • Spoon the batter into the prepared cups, filling each one three-quarters full. • Bake for 25–30 minutes, until risen and firm to the touch. • Transfer the muffin tin to a wire rack. Let cool completely before removing the cupcakes. • **Chocolate Hazelnut Frosting:** Melt the chocolate in a double boiler over barely simmering water, stirring until smooth. Remove from the heat and stir in the chocolate hazelnut spread. Let cool a little. • Spoon the mixture into a pastry bag fitted with a star nozzle and pipe a little on top of each cupcake. Sprinkle with the coarsely chopped hazelnuts.

CUPCAKES

2   cups (250 g) pecans, ground

1¼   cups (250 g) sugar

¼   cup (30 g) unsweetened cocoa powder, sifted

1   teaspoon baking powder

1   teaspoon ground cinnamon

⅛   teaspoon salt

4   large eggs, lightly beaten

½   cup (125 ml) unsalted butter, melted

1   teaspoon vanilla extract (essence)

1   teaspoon finely grated orange zest

    Pecan halves, to decorate

CHOCOLATE GANACHE

3   ounces (90 g) dark chocolate, coarsely chopped

⅓   cup (90 ml) light (single) cream

CHOCOLATE & PECAN CUPCAKES

Preheat the oven to 325°F (170°C/gas 3). • Line a standard 12-cup muffin tin with paper liners. • **Cupcakes:** Combine the ground pecans, sugar, cocoa, baking powder, cinnamon, and salt in a medium bowl. • Combine the eggs, butter, vanilla, and orange zest in a small bowl. • Pour the egg mixture into the mixed dry ingredients and stir until combined. • Spoon the batter into the prepared cups, filling each one three-quarters full. • Bake for 25–30 minutes, until risen and firm to the touch. • Transfer the muffin tin to a wire rack. Let cool completely before removing the cupcakes. • **Chocolate Ganache:** Melt the chocolate and cream in a double boiler over barely simmering water, stirring until smooth. Refrigerate until thickened, about 10 minutes. • Spread the chocolate ganache on top of each cupcake. • Cut the pecan halves in half lengthwise and arrange them meeting in the center and pointing outward on top of the cupcakes.

66 Make sure that the cocoa, baking powder, vanilla, and chocolate don't contain traces of gluten. Buy reputable brands that are clearly marked gluten-free.

MAKES: 12   PREPARATION: 20 MINUTES   COOKING: 25–30 MINUTES   LEVEL: 1

CUPCAKES

- 3 ounces (90 g) dark chocolate, coarsely chopped
- ⅓ cup (90 ml) light (single) cream
- ⅔ cup (100 g) all-purpose (plain) flour
- ½ cup (50 g) ground almonds
- 2 tablespoons unsweetened cocoa powder, sifted

- 1 teaspoon baking powder
- ⅛ teaspoon salt
- ⅓ cup (90 g) unsalted butter, softened
- 1 cup (200 g) sugar
- 2 large eggs
- 1 cup (150 g) fresh or frozen (thawed) raspberries

SUGARED RASPBERRIES

- 1 cup (150 g) fresh raspberries
- 1 large egg white, lightly beaten
- 2 tablespoons superfine (caster) sugar

CHOCOLATE BUTTERCREAM

- 3 ounces (90 g) dark chocolate
- ½ cup (125 g) unsalted butter, softened
- ¼ teaspoon vanilla extract (essence)
- ½ tablespoon milk
- 1 cup (150 g) confectioners' (icing) sugar

CHOCOLATE & RASPBERRY CUPCAKES

Preheat the oven to 325°F (170°C/gas 3). • Line a standard 12-cup muffin tin with paper liners. • **Cupcakes:** Melt the chocolate and cream in a double boiler over barely simmering water, stirring until smooth. Remove from the heat and let cool. • Combine the flour, ground almonds, cocoa, baking powder, and salt in a small bowl. • Beat the butter and sugar in a medium bowl with an electric mixer on medium-high speed until pale and creamy. • Add the eggs one at a time, beating until just blended after each addition. • With mixer on low speed, add the mixed dry ingredients and melted chocolate. • Stir the raspberries in by hand. • Spoon the batter into the prepared cups, filling each one three-quarters full. • Bake for 25–30 minutes, until golden brown and firm to the touch. • Transfer the muffin tin to a wire rack. Let cool completely before removing the cupcakes. • **Sugared Raspberries:** Line a baking sheet with parchment paper. • Brush each raspberry with egg white and roll in the sugar. Place the raspberries on the prepared sheet and leave to dry. • **Chocolate Buttercream:** Melt the chocolate in a double boiler over barely simmering water, stirring until smooth. Remove from the heat and let cool. • Beat the butter and vanilla in a medium bowl with an electric mixer on medium-high speed until pale and creamy. • Pour in the milk and cooled chocolate, beating until blended. Gradually add the sugar, beating until blended. • Spread the buttercream on top of each cupcake and top with sugared raspberries.

MAKES: 12 PREPARATION: 30 MINUTES COOKING: 25–30 MINUTES LEVEL: 2

CUPCAKES

- 3 ounces (90 g) white chocolate, coarsely chopped
- ⅓ cup (90 ml) light (single) cream
- 1 cup (150 g) all-purpose (plain) flour
- 1 teaspoon baking powder
- ⅛ teaspoon salt
- ⅓ cup (90 g) unsalted butter, softened

- 1 cup (200 g) sugar
- 1 teaspoon vanilla extract (essence)
- 2 large eggs
- 1 cup (150 g) strawberries, coarsely chopped, plus extra, sliced, to decorate

WHITE CHOCOLATE BUTTERCREAM

- 3 ounces (90 g) white chocolate
- ½ cup (125 g) salted butter, softened
- ¼ teaspoon vanilla extract (essence)
- ½ tablespoon milk
- 1 cup (150 g) confectioners' (icing) sugar

STRAWBERRY SHORTCAKE CUPCAKES

Preheat the oven to 325°F (170°C/gas 3). • Line a standard 12-cup muffin tin with paper liners. • **Cupcakes:** Melt the chocolate and cream in a double boiler over barely simmering water, stirring until smooth. Remove from the heat and let cool. • Combine the flour, baking powder, and salt in a small bowl. • Beat the butter, sugar, and vanilla in a medium bowl with an electric mixer on medium-high speed until pale and creamy. • Add the eggs one at a time, beating until just blended after each addition. • With mixer on low speed, add the mixed dry ingredients and melted chocolate. • Stir in the chopped strawberries by hand. • Spoon the batter into the prepared cups,

filling each one three-quarters full. • Bake for 25–30 minutes, until golden brown and firm to the touch. • Transfer the muffin tin to a wire rack. Let cool completely before removing the cupcakes. • **White Chocolate Buttercream:** Melt the chocolate in a double boiler over barely simmering water, stirring until smooth. Remove from the heat and let cool. • Beat the butter and vanilla in a medium bowl with an electric mixer on medium-high speed until creamy. • Pour in the milk and cooled chocolate, beating until blended. • Gradually add the confectioners' sugar, beating until blended. • Spread the buttercream on top of each cupcake and top with strawberry slices.

MAKES: 12 PREPARATION: 30 MINUTES COOKING: 25–30 MINUTES LEVEL: 1

CUPCAKES

3	ounces (90 g) dark chocolate, coarsely chopped
½	cup (125 ml) freshly squeezed orange juice
⅔	cup (100 g) all-purpose (plain) flour
½	cup (50 g) ground almonds
2	tablespoons unsweetened cocoa powder, sifted
1	teaspoon baking powder

⅛	teaspoon salt
⅓	cup (90 g) unsalted butter, softened
1	cup (200 g) firmly packed light brown sugar
1	teaspoon finely grated orange zest
2	large eggs
1	tablespoon orange marmalade
	Thin slices candied (glacé) orange, to decorate

JAFFA GANACHE

4	ounces (120 g) dark chocolate, coarsely chopped
¼	cup (60 ml) light (single) cream
2	teaspoons finely grated orange zest

JAFFA CUPCAKES

Preheat the oven to 325°F (170°C/gas 3). • Line a standard 12-cup muffin tin with paper liners. • **Cupcakes:** Melt the chocolate and orange juice in a double boiler over barely simmering water, stirring until smooth. Remove from the heat and let cool. • Combine the flour, ground almonds, cocoa, baking powder, and salt in a small bowl. • Beat the butter, brown sugar, and orange zest in a medium bowl with an electric mixer on medium-high speed until creamy. • Add the eggs one at a time, beating until just blended after each addition. • With mixer on low speed, add the mixed dry ingredients, melted chocolate, and marmalade. • Spoon the batter into the prepared cups, filling each one three-quarters full. • Bake for 25–30 minutes, until risen and firm to the touch. • Transfer the muffin tin to a wire rack. Let cool completely before removing the cupcakes. • **Jaffa Ganache:** Melt the chocolate and cream in a double boiler over barely simmering water, stirring until smooth. Remove from the heat and let cool and thicken. • Stir in the orange zest. • Spread over each cupcake and top with pieces of candied orange.

" *These cupcakes are named for Jaffa oranges which come from Israel. Almost seedless, Jaffa oranges are small and very sweet with an intense flavor.*

MAKES: 12 PREPARATION: 30 MINUTES COOKING: 25–30 MINUTES LEVEL: 1

CUPCAKES

- 4 ounces (120 g) dark chocolate, coarsely chopped
- ⅓ cup (90 ml) light (single) cream
- ⅔ cup (100 g) all-purpose (plain) flour
- ½ cup (50 g) ground hazelnuts
- 2 tablespoons unsweetened cocoa powder, sifted
- 1 teaspoon baking powder
- ⅛ teaspoon salt
- ⅓ cup (90 g) unsalted butter, softened
- 1 cup (200 g) sugar
- 2 large eggs
- 1 tablespoon coffee liqueur
- 1 tablespoon freeze-dried coffee granules, dissolved in 1 teaspoon boiling water

COFFEE CREAM

- 1 cup (250 ml) heavy (double) cream
- 3 tablespoons confectioners' (icing) sugar
- ½ tablespoon coffee liqueur
- 1 teaspoon freeze-dried coffee granules, dissolved in ¼ teaspoon boiling water

Grated chocolate, to decorate

100 MOCHA CUPCAKES

Preheat the oven to 350°F (180°C/gas 4).
• Line a standard 12-cup muffin tin with paper liners. • **Cupcakes:** Melt the chocolate and cream in a double boiler over barely simmering water, stirring until smooth. Remove from the heat and let cool. • Combine the flour, hazelnuts, cocoa, baking powder, and salt in a small bowl. • Beat the butter and sugar in a medium bowl with an electric mixer on medium-high speed until pale and creamy.
• Add the eggs one at a time, beating until just blended after each addition. • With mixer on low speed, add the mixed dry ingredients,

melted chocolate, coffee liqueur, and coffee.
• Spoon the batter into the prepared cups, filling each one three-quarters full. • Bake for 20–25 minutes, until risen and firm to the touch. • Transfer the muffin tin to a wire rack. Let cool completely before removing the cupcakes. • **Coffee Cream:** Whip the cream in a small bowl with an electric mixer until it begins to thicken. • Gradually add the confectioners' sugar, whisking until soft peaks form. Stir in the coffee liqueur and coffee.
• Place a dollop of cream on top of each cupcake and top with grated chocolate.

66 *These cupcakes are great at brunch or as a dessert. Serve with tiny cups of espresso coffee.*

MAKES: 12 PREPARATION: 20 MINUTES COOKING: 20–25 MINUTES LEVEL: 1

CUPCAKES

3	ounces (90 g) dark chocolate, coarsely chopped
1/3	cup (90 ml) light (single) cream
1	cup (150 g) all-purpose (plain) flour
2	tablespoons unsweetened cocoa powder, sifted
1	teaspoon baking powder
1/8	teaspoon salt
1/3	cup (90 g) unsalted butter, softened
1	cup (200 g) firmly packed light brown sugar
2	large eggs
2	tablespoons dark rum
2	medium overripe bananas, peeled and mashed, plus extra, sliced, to decorate

CHOCOLATE RUM GLAZE

1/2	cup (125 ml) heavy (double) cream
1/2	tablespoon unsalted butter, cubed
1	tablespoon light corn (golden) syrup
4	ounces (120 g) dark chocolate, coarsely chopped
1	tablespoon dark rum

RUM CREAM

2/3	cup (150 ml) heavy (double) cream
2	tablespoons confectioners' (icing) sugar
1/2	tablespoon dark rum

102

CHOCOLATE, BANANA & RUM CUPCAKES

Preheat the oven to 350°F (180°C/gas 4).
• Line a standard 12-cup muffin tin with paper liners. • **Cupcakes:** Melt the chocolate and cream in a double boiler over barely simmering water, stirring until smooth. Remove from the heat and let cool. • Combine the flour, cocoa, baking powder, and salt into a small bowl.
• Beat the butter and brown sugar in a medium bowl with an electric mixer on medium-high speed until creamy. • Add the eggs one at a time, beating until just blended after each addition. • With mixer on low speed, add the mixed dry ingredients, melted chocolate, and rum. • Stir the mashed banana in by hand.
• Spoon the batter into the prepared cups, filling each one three-quarters full. • Bake for

20–25 minutes, until risen and firm to the touch. • Transfer the muffin tin to a wire rack. Let cool completely before removing the cupcakes. • **Chocolate Rum Glaze:** Heat the cream, butter, and corn syrup in a small saucepan over low heat until the butter has melted. • Remove from the heat and add the chocolate, stirring until melted. Stir in the rum and set aside until cooled and slightly thickened. • **Rum Cream:** Whip the cream in a small bowl with an electric mixer until it begins to thicken. Gradually add the confectioners' sugar, whisking until soft peaks form. Stir in the rum. • Spread the chocolate glaze on top of each cupcake. Place a dollop of cream on each one and top with a slice of banana.

CUPCAKES

- 3 ounces (90 g) dark chocolate, coarsely chopped
- ⅓ cup (90 ml) light (single) cream
- 1 cup (150 g) all-purpose (plain) flour
- 3 tablespoons unsweetened cocoa powder, sifted
- 1 teaspoon baking powder
- ⅛ teaspoon salt
- ⅓ cup (90 g) unsalted butter, softened
- 1 cup (200 g) sugar
- 1 teaspoon vanilla extract (essence)
- 2 large eggs
- ¾ cup (135 g) dates, coarsely chopped, plus 6 extra, sliced, to decorate

CARAMEL SAUCE

- 3 tablespoons unsalted butter
- 3 tablespoons light (single) cream
- ⅓ cup (70 g) firmly packed dark brown sugar

104

STICKY CHOCOLATE DATE CUPCAKES

Preheat the oven to 325°F (170°C/gas 3). • Line a standard 12-cup muffin tin with paper liners. • **Cupcakes:** Melt the chocolate and cream in a double boiler over barely simmering water, stirring until smooth. Remove from the heat and let cool. • Combine the flour, cocoa, baking powder, and salt in a small bowl. • Beat the butter, sugar, and vanilla in a medium bowl with an electric mixer on medium-high speed until pale and creamy. • Add the eggs one at a time, beating until just blended after each addition. • With mixer on low speed, add the mixed dry ingredients and melted chocolate.

• Stir the chopped dates in by hand. • Spoon the batter into the prepared cups, filling each one three-quarters full. • Bake for 25–30 minutes, until risen and firm to the touch. • Transfer the muffin tin to a wire rack. Let cool completely before removing the cupcakes. • **Caramel Sauce:** Combine the butter, cream, and brown sugar in a small saucepan over medium heat. Cook, stirring constantly, until the sugar dissolves. Increase the heat to high and boil for 2 minutes. Remove from the heat and set aside to cool and thicken. • Top each cupcake with a date and a drizzle of sauce.

❝ *The caramel sauce adds an extra flourish to these delectable cupcakes. If you are feeling wicked, make a double-sized batch of sauce and go wild.*

MAKES: 12 PREPARATION: 30 MINUTES COOKING: 25–30 MINUTES LEVEL: 1

CUPCAKES

3	ounces (90 g) white chocolate, coarsely chopped
⅓	cup (90 ml) light (single) cream
1	cup (150 g) all-purpose (plain) flour
1	teaspoon baking powder
½	teaspoon ground cinnamon
⅛	teaspoon salt

⅓	cup (90 g) unsalted butter, softened
1	cup (200 g) sugar
1	teaspoon vanilla extract (essence)
2	large eggs
½	cup (125 g) fresh or frozen (thawed) blueberries
½	cup (75 g) fresh blueberries, to decorate

WHITE CHOCOLATE FROSTING

4	ounces (120 g) white chocolate, coarsely chopped
½	cup (125 ml) light (single) cream
3	tablespoons confectioners' (icing) sugar

WHITE CHOCOLATE & BLUEBERRY CUPCAKE

Preheat the oven to 325°F (170°C/gas 3). • Line a standard 12-cup muffin tin with paper liners. • **Cupcakes:** Melt the chocolate and cream in a double boiler over barely simmering water, stirring until smooth. Remove from the heat and let cool. • Combine the flour, baking powder, cinnamon, and salt in a small bowl. • Beat the butter, sugar, and vanilla in a medium bowl with an electric mixer on medium-high speed until pale and creamy. • Add the eggs one at a time, beating until just blended after each addition. • With mixer on low speed, add the mixed dry ingredients and melted chocolate. • Stir in the blueberries by hand. • Spoon the batter into the prepared cups, filling each one three-quarters full. • Bake for 25–30 minutes, until golden brown and firm to the touch. • Transfer the muffin tin to a wire rack. Let cool completely before removing the cupcakes. • **White Chocolate Frosting:** Melt the chocolate and cream in a double boiler over barely simmering water, stirring until smooth. • Remove from the heat and sift in the confectioners' sugar, stirring until combined. • Refrigerate until thickened, about 15 minutes. • Spread the frosting over the cupcakes and top with blueberries.

❝ White chocolate and blueberries go beautifully together.

CUPCAKES

3	ounces (90 g) dark chocolate, coarsely chopped
⅓	cup (90 ml) light (single) cream
1	cup (150 g) all-purpose (plain) flour
2	tablespoons unsweetened cocoa powder, sifted
1	teaspoon baking powder
⅛	teaspoon salt

⅓	cup (90 g) unsalted butter, softened
1	cup (200 g) sugar
2	large eggs
2	tablespoons cherry brandy
½	cup (125 g) drained maraschino cherries, coarsely chopped, plus 36 extra, to decorate

TOPPING

⅔	cup (150 ml) heavy (double) cream
2	tablespoons confectioners' (icing) sugar
½	tablespoon cherry brandy
3	ounces (90 g) dark chocolate, coarsely grated

BLACK FOREST CUPCAKES

Preheat the oven to 350°F (180°C/gas 4).
• Line a standard 12-cup muffin tin with paper liners. • **Cupcakes:** Melt the chocolate and cream in a double boiler over barely simmering water, stirring until smooth. Remove from the heat and let cool. • Combine the flour, cocoa, baking powder, and salt in a small bowl. • Beat the butter and sugar in a medium bowl with an electric mixer on medium-high speed until pale and creamy. • Add the eggs one at a time, beating until just blended after each addition. • With mixer on low speed, add the mixed dry ingredients, melted chocolate, and cherry brandy. • Spoon the batter into the prepared cups, filling each one three-quarters full. • Bake for 20–25 minutes, until risen and firm to the touch. • Transfer the muffin tin to a wire rack. Let cool completely before removing the cupcakes. • **Topping:** Whip the cream in a small bowl with an electric mixer until it begins to thicken. • Gradually add the confectioners' sugar, whisking until soft peaks form. Stir in the cherry brandy. • Put a dollop of cream and 3 cherries on top of each cupcake. Top with grated chocolate.

" *These cupcakes mimic the flavors of the famous Bavarian Black Forest cake. Serve with a tiny glass of kirsch or cherry brandy.*

MAKES: 12 PREPARATION: 30 MINUTES COOKING: 20–25 MINUTES LEVEL: 1

CUPCAKES

3	ounces (90 g) white chocolate, coarsely chopped
⅓	cup (90 ml) light (single) cream
1	cup (150 g) all-purpose (plain) flour
½	cup (50 g) ground pistachios
1	teaspoon baking powder

⅛	teaspoon salt
⅓	cup (90 g) unsalted butter, softened
1	cup (200 g) sugar
2	large eggs
2	tablespoons rose water
12	pink sugared roses, to decorate

ROSE FROSTING

½	cup (125 g) unsalted butter, softened
½	tablespoon rose water
1½	cups (225 g) confectioners' (icing) sugar

ENGLISH ROSE CUPCAKES

Preheat the oven to 325°F (170°C/gas 3). • Line a standard 12-cup muffin tin with paper liners. • **Cupcakes:** Melt the chocolate and cream in a double boiler over barely simmering water, stirring until smooth. Remove from the heat and let cool. • Combine the flour, pistachios, baking powder, and salt in a small bowl. • Beat the butter, sugar, and vanilla in a medium bowl with an electric mixer on medium-high speed until pale and creamy. • Add the eggs one at a time, beating until just blended after each addition. • With mixer on low speed, add the mixed dry ingredients, melted chocolate, and rose water. • Spoon the batter into the prepared cups, filling each one three-quarters full. • Bake for 25–30 minutes, until golden brown and firm to the touch. • Transfer the muffin tin to a wire rack. Let cool completely before removing the cupcakes. • **Rose Frosting:** Beat the butter and rose water in a small bowl using an electric mixer until light and fluffy. • Gradually add the confectioners' sugar, beating until fully incorporated. • Place the frosting in a pastry bag fitted with a star nozzle. Pipe a large rosette of rose frosting on top of each cupcake and top with a sugared rose.

Prepare these cupcakes for your mother on Mother's Day. Or make them for a friend who is getting married or celebrating a birthday or anniversary.

MAKES: 12   PREPARATION: 25 MINUTES   COOKING: 25–30 MINUTES   LEVEL: 1

CUPCAKES

3 ounces (90 g) dark chocolate, coarsely chopped
½ cup (125 ml) light (single) cream
1 cup (150 g) all-purpose (plain) flour
2 tablespoons unsweetened cocoa powder, sifted
1 teaspoon baking powder
⅛ teaspoon salt

⅓ cup (90 g) unsalted butter, softened
1 cup (200 g) sugar
1 teaspoon vanilla extract (essence)
2 large eggs, lightly beaten
6 Oreo cookies (biscuits), coarsely chopped

TOPPING

1 cup (250 ml) heavy (double) cream
2 tablespoons confectioners' (icing) sugar
2 Oreo cookies (biscuits), coarsely chopped

COOKIES & CREAM CUPCAKES

Preheat the oven to 325°F (170°C/gas 3). • Line a standard 12-cup muffin tin with paper liners. • **Cupcakes:** Melt the chocolate and cream in a double boiler over barely simmering water, stirring until smooth. Remove from the heat and let cool. • Combine the flour, cocoa, baking powder, and salt into a small bowl. • Beat the butter, sugar, and vanilla in a medium bowl with an electric mixer on medium-high speed, until pale and creamy. • Add the eggs one at a time, beating until just blended after each addition. • With mixer on low speed, add the mixed dry ingredients and melted chocolate. • Stir the Oreo cookies in by hand. • Spoon the batter into the prepared cups, filling each one three-quarters full. • Bake for 25–30 minutes, until risen and firm to the touch. • Transfer the muffin tin to a wire rack. Let cool completely before removing the cupcakes. • **Topping:** Whip the cream in a small bowl with an electric mixer until it begins to thicken. Gradually add the confectioners' sugar, whisking until soft peaks form. • Stir in the Oreo cookies and place a dollop of the cream on top of each cupcake.

66 *Oreo cookies are chocolate cookies sandwiched together with a cream filling. Replace the Oreos with another similar chocolate cookie if preferred.*

MAKES: 12 PREPARATION: 20 MINUTES COOKING: 25–30 MINUTES LEVEL: 1

CUPCAKES

2	cups (300 g) all-purpose (plain) flour
4	tablespoons unsweetened cocoa powder, sifted
1	teaspoon ground cinnamon
¼	teaspoon ground cloves
⅛	teaspoon salt
1	cup (250 g) unsalted butter

1	cup (200 g) firmly packed light brown sugar
½	teaspoon baking soda (bicarbonate of soda)
½	tablespoon warm water
1	cup (250 ml) milk
½	cup (90 g) macadamia nuts, coarsely chopped
½	cup (90 g) milk chocolate chips

TOPPING

¾	cup (125 g) confectioners' (icing) sugar
1½	tablespoons, unsweetened cocoa powder, sifted
1½	tablespoons water
½	teaspoon vanilla extract (essence)
⅓	cup (50 g) macadamia nuts, coarsely chopped and lightly toasted

CHOCOLATE & MACADAMIA CUPCAKES

Preheat the oven to 325°F (170°C/gas 3). • Line two standard 12-cup muffin tins with 18 paper liners. • Combine the flour, cocoa, cinnamon, cloves, and salt into a small bowl. • Beat the butter and brown sugar in a medium bowl with an electric mixer on medium-high speed until pale and creamy. • Dissolve the baking soda in the water and add to the butter mixture. • With mixer on low speed, add the mixed dry ingredients and milk. • Stir the macadamias and chocolate chips in by hand. • Spoon the batter into the prepared cups, filling each one three-quarters full. • Bake for 25–30 minutes, until risen and firm to the touch. • Transfer the muffin tins to a wire rack. Let cool completely before removing the cupcakes. • **Topping:** Combine the confectioners' sugar, cocoa, water, and vanilla in a small bowl, stirring until smooth. • Spread the frosting over the cupcake and top with macadamia nuts.

❝ These cupcakes are quick and easy to prepare. They don't contain egg so can be served to guests with egg allergies.

MAKES: 18 PREPARATION: 20 MINUTES COOKING: 25–30 MINUTES LEVEL: 1

CUPCAKES

- 6 ounces (180 g) dark chocolate, coarsely chopped
- ⅓ cup (90 ml) light (single) cream
- ⅔ cup (100 g) all-purpose (plain) flour
- ½ cup (50 g) ground almonds
- 2 tablespoons unsweetened cocoa powder, sifted
- 1 teaspoon baking powder
- ⅛ teaspoon salt
- ⅓ cup (90 g) unsalted butter, softened
- 1 cup (200 g) firmly packed light brown sugar
- 1 teaspoon peppermint extract (essence)
- 2 large eggs

PEPPERMINT BUTTER FROSTING

- ½ cup (125 g) unsalted butter, softened
- ½ teaspoon peppermint extract (essence)
- 1½ cups (225 g) confectioners' (icing) sugar

PEPPERMINT SLICE CUPCAKES

Preheat the oven to 350°F (180°C/gas 4).
• Line a standard 12-cup muffin tin with paper liners. • **Cupcakes:** Melt half the chocolate with the cream in a double boiler over barely simmering water, stirring until smooth. Remove from the heat and let cool. • Combine the flour, ground almonds, cocoa, baking powder, and salt in a small bowl. • Beat the butter, brown sugar, and peppermint in a medium bowl with an electric mixer on medium-high speed until creamy. • Add the eggs one at a time, beating until just blended after each addition. • With mixer on low speed, add the mixed dry ingredients and melted chocolate. • Put a tablespoon of the batter into the prepared cups. Place a chocolate square on top and cover with batter, filling each one three-quarters full. • Bake for 20–25 minutes, until golden brown and firm to the touch.
• Transfer the muffin tin to a wire rack. Let cool completely before removing the cupcakes.
• Melt the remaining chocolate in a double boiler over barely simmering water, stirring until smooth. Remove from the heat and let cool. • **Peppermint Butter Frosting:** Beat the butter and peppermint in a small bowl using an electric mixer until light and fluffy. Gradually add the confectioners' sugar, beating until fully incorporated. • Cut some of the crumb out of the top of each cupcake. Fill the hole with the buttercream and cover with a layer of cooled melted chocolate.

MAKES: 12 PREPARATION: 25 MINUTES COOKING: 20–25 MINUTES LEVEL: 2

CUPCAKES

- 1 ounce (30 g) dark chocolate, coarsely chopped
- 2 tablespoons light (single) cream
- 1 cup (150 g) all-purpose (plain) flour
- 1 teaspoon baking powder
- ⅛ teaspoon salt
- ⅓ cup (90 g) unsalted butter, softened

- 1 cup (200 g) sugar
- 1 teaspoon vanilla extract (essence)
- 2 large eggs
- 2 tablespoons milk
- 1 tablespoon unsweetened cocoa powder, sifted

CHOCOLATE AND VANILLA BUTTER FROSTING

- ½ cup (125 g) unsalted butter, softened
- ½ teaspoon vanilla extract (essence)
- 1½ cups (225 g) confectioners' (icing) sugar
- ¾ tablespoon unsweetened cocoa powder, sifted

CHOCOLATE SWIRL CUPCAKES

Preheat the oven to 325°F (170°C/gas 3). • Line a standard 12-cup muffin tin with paper liners. • **Cupcakes:** Melt the chocolate and cream in a double boiler over barely simmering water, stirring until smooth. Remove from the heat and let cool. • Combine the flour, baking powder, and salt in a small bowl. • Beat the butter, sugar, and vanilla in a medium bowl with an electric mixer on medium-high speed until pale and creamy. • Add the eggs one at a time, beating until just blended after each addition. • With mixer on low speed, add the mixed dry ingredients. • Divide the mixture between two bowls. Stir the milk into one batter and the melted chocolate and cocoa into the other. • Spoon the batters alternately into the prepared cups, filling each one three-quarters full. Create a swirl pattern through the batter using a skewer. • Bake for 25–30 minutes, until golden brown and firm to the touch. • Transfer the muffin tin to a wire rack. Let cool completely before removing the cupcakes. • **Chocolate and Vanilla Butter Frosting:** Beat the butter and vanilla in a small bowl using an electric mixer until light and fluffy. Gradually add the confectioners' sugar, beating until fully incorporated. • Divide the butter frosting between two bowls. Add the cocoa to one to make chocolate. Place alternate spoonfuls of vanilla and chocolate butter frosting into a pastry bag fitted with a star nozzle. Pipe a swirl on top of each cupcake.

MAKES: 12 PREPARATION: 30 MINUTES COOKING: 25–30 MINUTES LEVEL: 2

CUPCAKES

12 ounces (350 g) dark chocolate

¾ cup (180 g) unsalted butter, chopped

6 large eggs

1 cup (200 g) firmly packed light brown sugar

¼ cup (60 ml) maple syrup

1 cup (100 g) ground walnuts

⅓ cup (50 g) walnuts, coarsely chopped

10 walnut halves, to decorate

CHOCOLATE GLAZE

⅓ cup (90 ml) heavy (double) cream

½ tablespoon unsalted butter

½ tablespoon light corn (golden) syrup

3 ounces (90 g) dark chocolate, coarsely chopped

120

CHOCOLATE & WALNUT MUD CUPCAKES

Preheat the oven to 325°F (170°C/gas 3). • Line a standard 12-cup muffin tin with paper liners. • **Cupcakes:** Melt the chocolate and butter in a double boiler over barely simmering water, stirring until smooth. Remove from the heat and let cool. • Whisk the eggs, brown sugar, maple syrup, ground walnuts, and chopped walnuts in a medium bowl. • Pour in the chocolate and whisk until combined. • Spoon the batter into the prepared cups, filling each one three-quarters full. • Bake for 30–35 minutes, until risen and firm to the touch. • Transfer the muffin tin to a wire rack. Let cool completely before removing the cupcakes. • **Chocolate Glaze:** Heat the cream, butter, and syrup in a small saucepan over low heat until the butter has melted. Remove from the heat and add the chocolate, stirring until melted. Set aside until cooled and slightly thickened. • Spoon the glaze over each cupcake and top with a walnut half.

    These scrumptious cupcakes are intense in flavor and brownie-like in texture—a real treat for chocolate lovers. They are also gluten-free.

MAKES: 12 PREPARATION: 15 MINUTES COOKING: 30–35 MINUTES LEVEL: 1

CUPCAKES

½ teaspoon freeze-dried coffee granules
2 tablespoons dark rum
½ cup (90 g) raisins
2 tablespoons dark rum
3 ounces (90 g) dark chocolate, coarsely chopped
⅓ cup (90 ml) light (single) cream
1 cup (150 g) all-purpose (plain) flour

2 tablespoons unsweetened cocoa powder, sifted
1 teaspoon baking powder
⅛ teaspoon salt
⅓ cup (90 g) unsalted butter, softened
1 cup (200 g) firmly packed dark brown sugar
2 large eggs

CHOCOLATE RUM BUTTER FROSTING

½ cup (125 g) unsalted butter, softened
1½ tablespoons dark rum
1½ cups (225 g) confectioners' (icing) sugar
2 tablespoons unsweetened cocoa powder, sifted
Raisins, to decorate

CHOCOLATE RUM & RAISIN CUPCAKES

Preheat the oven to 325°F (170°C/gas 3). • Line a standard 12-cup muffin tin with paper liners. • **Cupcakes:** Combine the coffee, rum, and raisins in a small bowl and set aside to plump. • Melt the chocolate and cream in a double boiler over barely simmering water, stirring until smooth. Remove from the heat and let cool. • Combine the flour, cocoa, baking powder, and salt in a small bowl. • Beat the butter and brown sugar in a medium bowl with an electric mixer on medium-high speed until creamy. • Add the eggs one at a time, beating until just blended after each addition. • With mixer on low speed, add the mixed dry ingredients and melted chocolate. • Stir the raisins in by hand. • Spoon the batter into the prepared cups, filling each one three-quarters full. • Bake for 25–30 minutes, until risen and firm to the touch. • Transfer the muffin tin to a wire rack. Let cool completely before removing the cupcakes. • **Chocolate Rum Butter Frosting:** Beat the butter and rum in a small bowl using an electric mixer until light and fluffy. • Gradually add the confectioners' sugar and cocoa, beating until fully incorporated. • Spread the frosting on each cupcake and decorate with raisins around the outside border.

CUPCAKES

3   ounces (90 g) dark chocolate, coarsely chopped
⅓   cup (90 ml) light (single) cream
⅔   cup (100 g) all-purpose (plain) flour
¼   cup (50 g) malt powder, plus extra, to dust
2   tablespoons unsweetened cocoa powder, sifted

1   teaspoon baking powder
⅛   teaspoon salt
⅓   cup (90 g) unsalted butter, softened
1   cup (200 g) firmly packed light brown sugar
1   teaspoon vanilla extract (essence)
2   large eggs

CHOCOLATE FROSTING

3   ounces (90 g) dark chocolate, coarsely chopped
1   tablespoon unsalted butter, softened
⅓   cup (90 ml) heavy (double) cream
2   tablespoons confectioners' (icing) sugar

CHOCOLATE MALT CUPCAKES

Preheat the oven to 325°F (170°C/gas 3). • Line a standard 12-cup muffin tin with paper liners. • Melt the chocolate and cream in a double boiler over barely simmering water, stirring until smooth. Remove from the heat and let cool. • Combine the flour, malt, cocoa, baking powder, and salt in a small bowl. • Beat the butter, brown sugar, and vanilla in a medium bowl with an electric mixer on medium-high speed until creamy. • Add the eggs one at a time, beating until just blended after each addition. • With mixer on low speed, add the mixed dry ingredients and melted chocolate. • Spoon the batter into the prepared cups, fillin each one three-quarters full. • Bake for 25–30 minutes, until risen and firm to the touch. • Transfer the muffin tin to a wire rack. Let cool completely before removing the cupcakes. • **Chocolate Frosting:** Melt the chocolate, butte and cream in a double boiler over barely simmering water, stirring until smooth. Add the confectioners' sugar, stirring until smooth. Set aside to cool and thicken. • Spread the frosting on each cupcake and dust with malt powder.

" *Malt powder imparts a wonderful flavor to these cupcakes. It also helps them rise and gives them a good, fine crumb. Malt powder can bought at health food stores or from online suppliers.*

MAKES: 12 PREPARATION: 25 MINUTES COOKING: 25–30 MINUTES LEVEL: 1

CUPCAKES

3 ounces (90 g) dark chocolate, coarsely chopped

¼ cup (60 g) unsalted butter

1½ cups (225 g) all-purpose (plain) flour

¾ cup (150 g) firmly packed light brown sugar

2 tablespoons unsweetened cocoa powder, sifted

1½ teaspoons baking powder

1 teaspoon baking soda (bicarbonate of soda)

⅛ teaspoon salt

1 cup (250 ml) milk

1 cup (150 g) fresh or frozen and thawed mixed berries, plus extra fresh berries, to decorate

CHOCOLATE FROSTING

3 ounces (90 g) dark chocolate, coarsely chopped

1 tablespoon unsalted butter, softened

⅓ cup (90 ml) heavy (double) cream

2 tablespoons confectioners' (icing) sugar, to dust

CHOCOLATE BERRY CUPCAKES

EGG FREE

Preheat the oven to 325°F (170°C/gas 3). • Line a standard 12-cup muffin tin with paper liners. • **Cupcakes:** Melt the chocolate and butter in a double boiler over barely simmering water, stirring until smooth. • Combine the flour, brown sugar, cocoa, baking powder, baking soda, and salt in a medium bowl. • Pour the melted chocolate and milk into the mixed dry ingredients and mix until just combined. • Stir the 1 cup (150 g) mixed berries in by hand. • Spoon the batter into the prepared cups, filling each one three-quarters full. • Bake for 25–30 minutes, until risen and firm to the touch. • Transfer the muffin tin to a wire rack. Let cool completely before removing the cupcakes. • **Chocolate Frosting:** Melt the chocolate, butter, and cream in a double boiler over barely simmering water, stirring until smooth. Set aside to cool and thicken. • Spread the frosting over the cupcakes and top with extra berries. Dust with confectioners' sugar.

" These cupcakes are quick and easy to make. Decorate with a mixture of fresh red and black berries for a striking effect.

MAKES: 12 PREPARATION: 15 MINUTES COOKING: 25–30 MINUTES LEVEL: 1

CUPCAKES

- 4 ounces (120 g) dark chocolate, coarsely chopped
- ¼ cup (60 ml) light (single) cream
- ¾ cup (125 g) all-purpose (plain) flour
- 2 tablespoons unsweetened cocoa powder, sifted
- 1 teaspoon baking powder

- 1 teaspoon allspice or pumpkin pie spice
- ⅛ teaspoon salt
- ¼ cup (60 ml) sunflower oil
- ½ cup (100 g) firmly packed light brown sugar
- 2 large eggs
- 4 ounces (120 g) grated butternut pumpkin

CHOCOLATE GANACHE

- 3 ounces (90 g) dark chocolate, coarsely chopped
- ⅓ cup (90 ml) light (single) cream

CHOCOLATE & PUMPKIN CUPCAKES

Preheat the oven to 350°F (180°C/gas 4).
• Line a standard 12-cup muffin tin with paper liners. • **Cupcakes:** Melt the chocolate and cream in a double boiler over barely simmering water, stirring until smooth. Remove from the heat and let cool. • Combine the flour, cocoa, baking powder, spice, and salt in a small bowl. • Combine the oil, brown sugar, and eggs in a medium bowl. • Stir in the pumpkin. • Add the mixed dry ingredients and chocolate, stirring well to combine. • Spoon the batter into the prepared cups, filling each one three-quarters full. • Bake for 20–25 minutes, until risen and firm to the touch. • Transfer the muffin tin to a wire rack. Let cool completely before removing the cupcakes. • **Chocolate Ganache:** Melt the chocolate and cream in a double boiler over barely simmering water, stirring until smooth. Refrigerate until thickened, about 15 minutes. • Spread the chocolate ganache over the cupcakes.

66 *These tasty muffins are great in fall and winter when fresh pumpkin is available. They are perfect at Thanksgiving.*

MAKES: 12 PREPARATION: 20 MINUTES + 15 MINUTES TO CHILL COOKING: 20–25 MINUTES LEVEL: 1

CUPCAKES

- 3 ounces (90 g) dark chocolate, coarsely chopped
- ⅓ cup (90 ml) light (single) cream
- 1 cup (150 g) all-purpose (plain) flour
- 2 tablespoons unsweetened cocoa powder, sifted
- 1 teaspoon baking powder

- ⅛ teaspoon salt
- ⅓ cup (90 g) unsalted butter, softened
- 1 cup (200 g) sugar
- 1 teaspoon vanilla extract (essence)
- 2 large eggs
- 12 caramel filled chocolate squares
  Caramel sauce, to decorate

CHOCOLATE BUTTERCREAM

- 3 ounces (90 g) milk chocolate, coarsely chopped
- ½ cup (125 g) unsalted butter, softened
- ¼ teaspoon vanilla extract (essence)
- ½ tablespoon milk
- ½ cup (75 g) confectioners' (icing) sugar

CHOCOLATE CARAMEL CUPCAKES

Preheat the oven to 325°F (170°C/gas 3). • Line a standard 12-cup muffin tin with paper liners. • **Cupcakes:** Melt the chocolate and cream in a double boiler over barely simmering water, stirring until smooth. Remove from the heat and let cool. • Combine the flour, cocoa, baking powder, and salt in a small bowl. • Beat the butter, sugar, and vanilla in a medium bowl with an electric mixer on medium-high speed until pale and creamy. • Add the eggs one at a time, beating until just blended after each addition. • With mixer on low speed, add the mixed dry ingredients and melted chocolate. • Put half the batter into the prepared cups. Place a chocolate square in the center and cover with the remaining batter, filling each one three-quarters full. • Bake for 25–30 minutes, until risen and firm to the touch.

• Transfer the muffin tin to a wire rack. Let coo completely before removing the cupcakes. • **Chocolate Buttercream:** Melt the chocolate in a double boiler over barely simmering water stirring until smooth. Remove from the heat and let cool. • Beat the butter and vanilla in a medium bowl with an electric mixer on medium-high speed until pale and creamy. • Pour in the milk and cooled chocolate, beating until blended. Gradually add the confectioners' sugar, beating until blended. • Spread three-quarters of the buttercream ove the cupcakes. • Spoon the remaining buttercream into a pastry bag fitted with a sta shaped nozzle. Pipe a border of small stars around the cupcakes. • Drizzle the caramel sauce in a zigzag pattern inside the border.

MAKES: 12 PREPARATION: 20 MINUTES COOKING: 25–30 MINUTES LEVEL: 2

CUPCAKES

- 3 ounces (90 g) dark chocolate, coarsely chopped
- ½ cup (125 ml) light (single) cream
- 1 cup (150 g) all-purpose (plain) flour
- 2 tablespoons unsweetened cocoa powder, sifted
- 1 teaspoon chilli powder
- 1 teaspoon baking powder
- ⅛ teaspoon salt
- ⅓ cup (90 g) unsalted butter, softened
- 1 cup (200 g) sugar
- 1 teaspoon vanilla extract (essence)
- 2 large eggs

CHOCOLATE GANACHE

- 3 ounces (90 g) dark chocolate, coarsely chopped
- ⅓ cup (90 ml) light (single) cream
- ½ teaspoon chilli powder

TO DECORATE

- ¾ cup (125 g) confectioners' (icing) sugar
- 1½ tablespoons water
- ⅛ teaspoon red food coloring

CHOCOLATE CHILLI CUPCAKES

Preheat the oven to 325°F (170°C/gas 3). • Line a standard 12-cup muffin tin with paper liners. • **Cupcakes:** Melt the chocolate and cream in a double boiler over barely simmering water, stirring until smooth. Remove from the heat and let cool. • Combine the flour, cocoa, chilli powder, baking powder, and salt in a small bowl. • Beat the butter, sugar, and vanilla in a medium bowl with an electric mixer on medium-high speed until pale and creamy. • Add the eggs one at a time, beating until just blended after each addition. • With mixer on low speed, add the mixed dry ingredients and melted chocolate. • Spoon the batter into the prepared cups, filling each one three-quarters full. • Bake for 25–30 minutes, until risen and firm to the touch. • Transfer the muffin tin to a wire rack. Let cool completely before removing the cupcakes. • Prepare a small paper piping bag: Cut a piece of parchment paper into an 8 x 12 x 14-inch (20 x 30 x 35-cm) triangle. Curl the paper into a cone-shape, forming the cone's point mid way along the long side. Tighten the cone and tuck the top flap inside the cone, securing with tape. • **Chocolate Ganache:** Melt the chocolate, cream, and chilli powder in a double boiler over barely simmering water, stirring until smooth. Refrigerate until thickened, about 15 minutes. • Spread the chocolate ganache on each cupcake. • **To Decorate:** Combine the confectioners' sugar and water in a small bowl stirring until smooth. Add red food coloring to create a bright red frosting. • Spoon the frosting into the prepared bag and cut the tip off, using scissors or a sharp knife. Pipe a border around the cupcakes and a chilli design in the center.

MAKES: 12 PREPARATION: 30 MINUTES + 15 MINUTES TO CHILL COOKING: 25–30 MINUTES LEVEL: 2

CUPCAKES

3   ounces (90 g) dark chocolate, coarsely chopped
⅓ cup (90 ml) light (single) cream
1   cup (150 g) all-purpose (plain) flour
2   tablespoons unsweetened cocoa powder, sifted

1   teaspoon baking powder
⅛ teaspoon salt
⅓ cup (90 g) unsalted butter, softened
1   cup (200 g) sugar
1   teaspoon vanilla extract (essence)
2   large eggs

MERINGUE

3   large egg whites
¼ teaspoon cream of tartar
⅓ cup (70 g) superfine (caster) sugar

CHOCOLATE MERINGUE CUPCAKES

Preheat the oven to 325°F (170°C/gas 3). • Line a standard 12-cup muffin tin with paper liners. • **Cupcakes:** Melt the chocolate and cream in a double boiler over barely simmering water, stirring until smooth. Remove from the heat and let cool. • Combine the flour, cocoa, baking powder, and salt in a small bowl. • Beat the butter, sugar, and vanilla in a medium bowl with an electric mixer on medium-high speed until pale and creamy. • Add the eggs one at a time, beating until just blended after each addition. • With mixer on low speed, add the mixed dry ingredients and melted chocolate. • Spoon the batter into the prepared cups, filling each one three-quarters full. • Bake for 25–30 minutes, until risen and firm to the touch. • Transfer the muffin tin to a wire rack. Let cool completely before removing the cupcakes. • Increase the oven temperature to 450°F (230°C/gas 8). **Meringue:** Beat the egg whites and cream of tartar in a medium bowl with an electric mixer on medium speed until soft peaks form. Gradually add the sugar, whisking until it is all incorporated and meringue is thick and glossy. • Spoon the meringue into a pastry bag fitted with a star shaped nozzle. Pipe the meringue on top of the cupcakes. • Bake in the oven until golden, about 5 minutes.

CUPCAKES

3	ounces (90 g) dark chocolate, coarsely chopped
⅓	cup (90 ml) light (single) cream
1	cup (150 g) all-purpose (plain) flour
2	tablespoons unsweetened cocoa powder, sifted, plus extra, to dust
1½	teaspoons allspice or pumpkin pie spice

1	teaspoon baking powder
⅛	teaspoon salt
⅓	cup (90 g) unsalted butter, softened
1	cup (200 g) sugar
1	teaspoon vanilla extract (essence)
2	large eggs

SPICED BUTTERCREAM

3	ounces (90 g) white chocolate, coarsely chopped
½	cup (125 g) unsalted butter, softened
¼	teaspoon vanilla extract (essence)
1	teaspoon allspice or pumpkin pie spice
½	tablespoon milk
½	cup (75 g) confectioners' (icing) sugar

CHOCOLATE SPICE CUPCAKES

Preheat the oven to 325°F (170°C/gas 3). • Line a standard 12-cup muffin tin with paper liners. • **Cupcakes:** Melt the chocolate and cream in a double boiler over barely simmering water, stirring until smooth. Remove from the heat and let cool. • Combine the flour, cocoa, spice, baking powder, and salt in a small bowl. • Beat the butter, sugar, and vanilla in a medium bowl with an electric mixer on medium-high speed, until pale and creamy. • Add the eggs one at a time, beating until just blended after each addition. • With mixer on low speed, add the mixed dry ingredients and melted chocolate. • Spoon the batter into the prepared cups, filling each one three-quarters full. • Bake for 25–30 minutes, until risen and firm to the touch. • Transfer the muffin tin to a wire rack. Let cool completely before removing the cupcakes. • **Spiced Buttercream:** Melt the chocolate in a double boiler over barely simmering water, stirring until smooth. Remove from the heat and let cool. • Beat the butter, vanilla, and spice in a medium bowl with an electric mixer on medium-high speed, until pale and creamy. • Pour in the milk and cooled chocolate, beating until blended. Gradually add the confectioners' sugar, beating until blended. • Spoon the buttercream into a pastry bag fitted with a plain nozzle and pipe a zigzag pattern back and forth on top of the cupcakes. Dust with cocoa.

MAKES: 12 PREPARATION: 25 MINUTES COOKING: 25–30 MINUTES LEVEL: 1

10	ounces (300 g) dark chocolate, coarsely chopped, plus extra, grated, to decorate	½	cup (100 g) firmly packed light brown sugar	1	teaspoon baking powder flour
1¼	cups (300 g) unsalted butter	1	teaspoon vanilla extract (essence)	½	cup (125 ml) heavy (double) cream
5	large eggs	¾	cup (125 g) all-purpose (plain) flour		

CHOCOLATE MUD CUPCAKES

Preheat the oven to 350°F (180°C/gas 4).
• Line a standard 12-cup muffin tin with paper liners. • Melt the chocolate and butter in a double boiler over barely simmering water, stirring until smooth. • Beat the eggs, brown sugar, and vanilla in a medium bowl with an electric mixer on medium-high speed until creamy. • Fold in the flour, baking powder, and melted chocolate by hand, until just combined.

• Spoon the batter into the prepared cups, filling each one three-quarters full. • Bake for 20 minutes, until risen and firm to the touch.
• Transfer the muffin tin to a wire rack. Let cool completely before removing the cupcakes.
• Whip the cream in a small bowl using an electric mixer on medium speed until soft peaks form. • Spoon a little whipped cream onto each cupcake. Top with grated chocolate.

66 *These rich muddy chocolate cupcakes make a great desert. If liked, serve warm with a scoop of vanilla ice cream.*

MAKES: 12 PREPARATION: 15 MINUTES COOKING: 20 MINUTES LEVEL: 1

PINE NUT PRALINE

¾ cup (150 g) superfine (caster) sugar
3 tablespoons water
¾ cup (135 g) pine nuts

CUPCAKES

3 ounces (90 g) dark chocolate, coarsely chopped
⅓ cup (90 ml) light (single) cream
1 cup (150 g) all-purpose (plain) flour
2 tablespoons unsweetened cocoa powder, sifted
1 teaspoon baking powder
⅛ teaspoon salt
⅓ cup (90 g) unsalted butter, softened
1 cup (200 g) sugar
1 teaspoon vanilla extract (essence)
2 large eggs

CHOCOLATE BUTTERCREAM

3 ounces (90 g) milk chocolate, coarsely chopped
½ cup (125 g) unsalted butter, softened
¼ teaspoon vanilla extract (essence)
½ tablespoon milk
½ cup (75 g) confectioners' (icing) sugar

140 CHOCOLATE & NUT PRALINE CUPCAKES

Preheat the oven to 325°F (170°C/gas 3). • Line a standard 12-cup muffin tin with paper liners. Line a baking sheet with parchment paper. **Pine Nut Praline:** Place the sugar and water in a small pan and gently heat until melted and pale gold, 5–10 minutes. Add the pine nuts and cook, stirring, for 1 minute. • Pour onto the prepared sheet and leave to harden for 20 minutes. • Break half the hardened praline into small shards and reserve for decorating. Process the other half into fine crumbs. • **Cupcakes:** Melt the chocolate and cream in a double boiler over barely simmering water, stirring until smooth. Remove from the heat and let cool. • Combine the flour, cocoa, baking powder, and salt in a small bowl. • Beat the butter, sugar, and vanilla in a medium bowl with an electric mixer on medium-high speed until pale and creamy. • Add the eggs one at a time, beating until just blended after each addition. • With mixer on low speed, add the mixed dry ingredients and melted chocolate. • Stir the praline crumbs in by hand. • Put a tablespoon of the batter into the prepared cups. Place a chocolate square on top and cover with batter, filling each one three-quarters full. • Bake for 25–30 minutes, until golden brown and firm to the touch. • Transfer the muffin tin to a wire rack. Let cool completely before removing the cupcakes. • **Chocolate Buttercream:** Melt the chocolate in a double boiler over barely simmering water, stirring until smooth. Remove from the heat and let cool. • Beat the butter and vanilla in a medium bowl with an electric mixer on medium-high speed until pale and creamy. • Pour in the milk and cooled chocolate, beating until blended. Gradually add the sugar, beating until blended. • Spoon the buttercream into a pastry bag fitted with a star shaped nozzle and pipe onto cupcakes. • Decorate with shards of pine nut praline.

MAKES: 12 PREPARATION: 30 MINUTES COOKING: 30–40 MINUTES LEVEL: 2

CUPCAKES
- ½ cup (60 g) amaranth flour
- ¾ cup (125 g) rice flour
- ¼ cup (30 g) unsweetened cocoa powder
- 1 tablespoon xanthan gum
- 1 teaspoon baking soda (bicarbonate of soda)
- ⅛ teaspoon salt
- 2 large eggs
- ¾ cup (150 g) firmly packed light brown sugar
- ½ cup (125 ml) vegetable oil
- ¼ cup (60 ml) milk
- 4 ounces (125 g) canned strawberries, halved
- ½ cup (90 g) white chocolate chips

CHOCOLATE STRAWBERRIES
- 3 ounces (90 g) dark chocolate
- 12 medium fresh strawberries

WHITE CHOCOLATE GANACHE
- 3 ounces (90 g) white chocolate, coarsely chopped
- ⅓ cup (90 ml) light (single) cream

CHOCOLATE & STRAWBERRY CUPCAKES

GLUTEN FREE

Preheat the oven to 325°F (170°C/gas 3). • Line a standard 12-cup muffin tin with paper liners. • **Cupcakes:** Sift both flours, cocoa powder, xanthan gum, baking soda, and salt into a medium bowl. • Beat the eggs in a medium bowl with an electric mixer on medium-high speed until pale and frothy. • Add the brown sugar, oil, and milk and whisk until incorporated. • With mixer on low speed, add the mixed dry ingredients and milk. • Stir the strawberries and chocolate chips in by hand. • Spoon the batter into the prepared cups, filling each one three-quarters full. • Bake for 25–30 minutes, until risen and firm to the touch. • Transfer the muffin tin to a wire rack. Let cool completely before removing the cupcakes. • Line a baking sheet with parchment paper. • **Chocolate Strawberries:** Melt the dark chocolate in a double boiler over barely simmering water, stirring until smooth. Dip the strawberries into the chocolate and place on the prepared baking sheet to set. • **White Chocolate Ganache:** Melt the chocolate and cream in a double boiler over barely simmering water, stirring until smooth. • Refrigerate until thickened, about 15 minutes. • Spread the ganache on top of each cupcake and top with strawberries.

children's
cupcakes

CUPCAKES
1¼ cups (180 g) whole-wheat (wholemeal) flour
1 teaspoon baking powder
1 teaspoon ground nutmeg
½ teaspoon baking soda (bicarbonate of soda)
½ cup (125 g) low-fat dairy-free spread

½ cup (100 g) firmly packed light brown sugar
1 teaspoon vanilla extract (essence)
2 large eggs
½ cup (125 ml) low-fat yogurt
2 medium overripe bananas, mashed

TO DECORATE
½ cup (125 ml) low-fat yogurt
1 small banana, sliced
3 tablespoons chopped nuts
2 ounces (60 g) dark chocolate, melted

146 BANANA SPLIT CUPCAKES

Preheat the oven to 350°F (180°C/gas 4). • Line a standard 12-cup muffin tin with paper liners. • **Cupcakes:** Combine the flour, baking powder, nutmeg, and baking soda in a small bowl. • Beat the low-fat spread, brown sugar, and vanilla in a medium bowl with an electric mixer on medium-high speed until creamy. • Add the eggs one at a time, beating until just blended after each addition. • With mixer on low speed, add the mixed dry ingredients and yogurt. • Stir the banana in by hand. • Spoon the batter into the prepared cups, filling each one three-quarters full. • Bake for 20–25 minutes, until golden brown and firm to the touch. • Transfer the muffin tin to a wire rack. Let cool completely before removing the cupcakes. • **To Decorate:** Put a dollop of yogurt on each cupcake. Arrange slices of banana on top. Sprinkle with nuts and drizzle with the melted chocolate.

Made with bananas and yogurt, these make a healthy after-school snack.

MAKES: 12 PREPARATION: 15 MINUTES COOKING: 20–25 MINUTES LEVEL: 1

CUPCAKES

1½	cups (225 g) all-purpose (plain) flour
¾	cup (150 g) sugar
3	tablespoons unsweetened cocoa powder, sifted
1½	teaspoons baking powder
1	teaspoon baking soda (bicarbonate of soda)
⅛	teaspoon salt
½	cup (125 g) unsalted butter, melted
1	cup (250 ml) milk
1	teaspoon vanilla extract (essence)

BUTTER FROSTING

½	cup (125 g) unsalted butter, softened
½	teaspoon vanilla extract (essence)
1½	cups (225 g) confectioners' (icing) sugar

TO DECORATE

	Black strap liquorice, to decorate
12	red candy-coated buttons, to decorate
12	orange candy-coated buttons, to decorate
12	green candy-coated buttons, to decorate
1	ounce (30 g) dark chocolate, melted

TRAFFIC LIGHT CUPCAKES

Preheat the oven to 350°F (180°C/gas 4). • Line a standard 12-cup muffin tin with paper liners. • **Cupcakes:** Combine the flour, sugar, cocoa, baking powder, baking soda, and salt in a small bowl. • Combine the butter, milk, and vanilla in a small bowl. • Add the butter mixture to the dry ingredients, mixing well to combine. • Spoon the batter into the prepared cups, filling each one three-quarters full. • Bake for 20–25 minutes, until golden brown and firm to the touch. • Transfer the muffin tin to a wire rack. Let cool completely before removing the cupcakes. • **Butter Frosting:** Beat the butter and vanilla in a small bowl using an electric mixer until creamy. • Gradually add the confectioners' sugar until combined. Spread on top of the cupcakes. • **To Decorate:** Cut the liquorice strips into rectangles. • Place a small amount of melted chocolate on the back of the candy-coated buttons and stick onto the liquorice strips, with colors in order of a traffic light. • Stick the "traffic lights" on top of the cupcakes using a little melted chocolate to hold in place, if necessary.

Children will enjoy helping to make these cupcakes.

MAKES: 12 PREPARATION: 30 MINUTES COOKING: 20–25 MINUTES LEVEL: 2

CUPCAKES

½ cup (75 g) all-purpose (plain) flour

½ cup (75 g) self-rising flour

½ cup (100 g) firmly packed dark brown sugar

4 tablespoons unsweetened cocoa powder, sifted

¼ teaspoon baking soda (bicarbonate of soda)

⅛ teaspoon salt

⅓ cup (90 g) unsalted butter, softened

1 large egg

1 teaspoon vanilla extract (essence)

¼ cup (60 ml) milk

TO DECORATE

1½ cups (225 g) confectioners' (icing) sugar

2½ tablespoons water

⅛ teaspoon yellow food coloring

48 red candy-coated buttons

24 small, blue candy-coated buttons

Black strap liquorice, cut into thin strips

BERTIE BEETLE CUPCAKES

Preheat the oven to 350°F (180°C/gas 4).
• Line a standard 12-cup muffin tin with paper liners. • **Cupcakes:** Combine both flours, sugar, cocoa, baking soda, and salt in a small bowl.
• Beat the butter, egg, and vanilla in a medium bowl with an electric mixer on low speed until combined. • Add the mixed dry ingredients and milk and beat on low speed until well mixed.
• Spoon the batter into the prepared cups, filling each one three-quarters full. • Bake for 20–25 minutes, until risen and firm to the touch. • Transfer the muffin tin to a wire rack. Let cool completely before removing the cupcakes. • **To Decorate:** Combine the confectioners' sugar and water in a small bowl, stirring until smooth. Add yellow food coloring to create a bright yellow frosting and spread over the cupcakes. • Before it sets, lay a strip of liquorice three-quarters of the way down the center of each cupcake. Place two red candy coated buttons on either side of the strip. Curve another strip of liquorice at the end of the center line, to create an outline for the beetle's head. Place 2 blue candy-coated buttons for eyes and put short liquorice strips for the antennas. Refer to photograph.

66 *If you don't have self-rising flour on hand, substitute with the same quantity of all-purpose (plain) flour and ½ teaspoon of baking powder.*

MAKES: 12 PREPARATION: 30 MINUTES COOKING: 20–25 MINUTES LEVEL: 2

CUPCAKES

1⅓	cups (200 g) all-purpose (plain) flour	1	teaspoon vanilla extract (essence)		
1½	teaspoons baking powder	2	large eggs		
⅛	teaspoon salt	½	cup (125 ml) milk		
½	cup (125 g) unsalted butter, softened				
1	cup (200 g) firmly packed light brown sugar				

TO DECORATE

1½ cups (225 g) confectioners' (icing) sugar
2½ tablespoons water
⅛ teaspoon red food coloring
⅛ teaspoon black food coloring

SPIDERMAN CUPCAKES

Preheat the oven to 350°F (180°C/gas 4).
• Line a standard 12-cup muffin tin with paper liners. • **Cupcakes:** Combine the flour, baking powder, and salt in a small bowl. • Beat the butter, sugar, and vanilla in a medium bowl with an electric mixer on medium-high speed until creamy. • Add the eggs one at a time, beating until just blended after each addition. • With mixer on low speed, add the mixed dry ingredients, alternating with the milk. • Spoon the batter into the prepared cups, filling each one three-quarters full. • Bake for 20–25 minutes, until golden brown and firm to the touch. • Transfer the muffin tin to a wire rack. Let cool completely before removing the cupcakes. • Prepare a small paper piping bag: Cut a piece of parchment paper into an 8 x 12 x 14-inch (20 x 30 x 35-cm) triangle. Curl the paper into a cone-shape, forming the cone's point mid way along the long side. Tighten the cone and tuck the top flap inside the cone, securing with tape.• **To Decorate:** Combine the confectioners' sugar and water in a small bowl, stirring until smooth. Transfer a quarter of the mixture to a small bowl and add a few drops of black food coloring to create a black frosting. • Add red food coloring to the remaining mixture, stirring to create a red frosting. • Spread the red frosting over the cup cakes. Spoon the black frosting into the prepared bag and cut the tip off, using scissors or a sharp knife. • Put a dot of black frosting in the center of each cupcake and then pipe three circles ¼ inch (5 mm) apart. Using a skewer, draw a line from the dot to the outside edge of the cake. Repeat 6 or 8 times to create a spider's web pattern. Refer to photograph.

MAKES: 12 PREPARATION: 30 MINUTES COOKING: 20–25 MINUTES LEVEL: 2

CUPCAKES

1¼ cups (180 g) all-purpose (plain) flour
⅓ cup (50 g) cornstarch (cornflour)
1½ teaspoons baking powder
1 teaspoon ground cinnamon
⅛ teaspoon salt
½ cup (125 g) unsalted butter, softened

¾ cup (150 g) sugar
1 teaspoon vanilla extract (essence)
2 large eggs
½ cup (125 ml) milk
1 cup (150 g) fresh or frozen (thawed) strawberries
  Colored sugar crystals, to decorate

PINK BUTTERCREAM

3 ounces (90 g) white chocolate
½ cup (125 g) unsalted butter, softened
¼ teaspoon vanilla extract (essence)
½ tablespoon milk
1 cup (150 g) confectioners' (icing) sugar
⅛ teaspoon pink food coloring

FAIRY DUST CUPCAKES

Preheat the oven to 350°F (180°C/gas 4). • Line a standard 12-cup muffin tin with paper liners. • **Cupcakes:** Combine the flour, cornstarch, baking powder, cinnamon, and salt in a small bowl. • Beat the butter, sugar, and vanilla in a medium bowl with an electric mixer on medium-high speed until pale and creamy. • Add the eggs one at a time, beating until just blended after each addition. • With mixer on low speed, add the mixed dry ingredients, alternating with the milk. • Stir the strawberries in by hand. • Spoon the batter into the prepared cups, filling each one three-quarters full. • Bake for 20–25 minutes, until golden brown and firm to the touch. • Transfer the muffin tin to a wire rack. Let cool completely before removing the cupcakes. • **Pink Buttercream:** Melt the chocolate in a double boiler over barely simmering water, stirring until smooth. Remove from the heat and let cool. • Beat the butter and vanilla in a medium bowl with an electric mixer on medium-high speed until pale and creamy. • With mixer on low speed, pour in the milk and cooled chocolate, beating until blended. Gradually add the confectioners' sugar, beating until blended. Add a few drops of pink food coloring, stirring to create a light pink color. • Spoon the buttercream into a pastry bag fitted with a star-shaped nozzle. Pipe small rosettes over the top of each cupcake and sprinkle with colored sugar.

MAKES: 12 PREPARATION: 35 MINUTES COOKING: 20–25 MINUTES LEVEL: 2

CUPCAKES

¾ cup (120 g) organic coconut milk powder (see note below)

1 cup (150 g) all-purpose (plain) flour

1 teaspoon baking powder

⅛ teaspoon salt

½ cup (125 g) dairy-free margarine

1 cup (200 g) sugar

1 teaspoon vanilla extract (essence)

4 large eggs

TOPPING

½ cup (125 ml) vanilla soy yogurt

1 tablespoon passion fruit pulp, strained

Confectioners' (icing) sugar, to dust

COCONUT BUTTERFLY CUPCAKES

DAIRY FREE

Preheat the oven to 325°F (170°C/gas 3). • Line a standard 12-cup muffin tin with paper liners. • **Cupcakes:** Combine the coconut milk powder, flour, baking powder, and salt into a medium bowl. • Beat the dairy-free margarine, sugar, and vanilla in a medium bowl with an electric mixer on medium-high speed until creamy. • Add the eggs one at a time, beating until just blended after each addition. • With mixer on low speed, add the mixed dry ingredients. • Spoon the batter into the prepared cups, filling each one three-quarters full. • Bake for 25–30 minutes, until golden brown and firm to the touch. • Transfer the muffin tin to a wire rack. Let cool completely before removing the cupcakes. • **Topping:** Combine the yogurt and passion fruit pulp in a small bowl. • Cut a small circle about ½ inch (1 cm) deep from the top of each cupcake. Cut each top in half and set aside. • Spoon the soy yogurt mixture into the hollows. Arrange pairs of the cupcake tops in the yogurt at an angle to resemble butterfly wings. • Dust with confectioners' sugar.

66 *Organic coconut milk powder is available at health food stores and from online suppliers. Some coconut milk powders contain traces of milk protein. Read the package labeling carefully and always buy reputable brands.*

MAKES: 12 PREPARATION: 25 MINUTES COOKING: 25–30 MINUTES LEVEL: 1

CUPCAKES

1½ cups (225 g) all-purpose (plain) flour

3 tablespoons unsweetened cocoa powder, sifted

1½ teaspoons baking powder

⅛ teaspoon salt

½ cup (125 g) unsalted butter, softened

¾ cup (150 g) firmly packed light brown sugar

1 teaspoon vanilla extract (essence)

2 large eggs

½ cup (125 ml) milk

½ cup (90 g) milk chocolate chips, melted, to decorate

BUTTER FROSTING

½ cup (125 g) unsalted butter, softened

½ teaspoon vanilla extract (essence)

1½ cups (225 g) confectioners' (icing) sugar

1 tablespoon unsweetened cocoa powder, sifted

SOCCER BALL CUPCAKE

Preheat the oven to 350°F (180°C/gas 4).
• Line a standard 12-cup muffin tin with paper liners. • **Cupcakes:** Combine the flour, cocoa, baking powder, and salt in a small bowl.
• Beat the butter, sugar, and vanilla in a medium bowl with an electric mixer on medium-high speed until creamy. • Add the eggs one at a time, beating until just blended after each addition. • With mixer on low speed, add the mixed dry ingredients, alternating with the milk. • Spoon the batter into the prepared cups, filling each one three-quarters full. • Bake for 20–25 minutes, until risen and firm to the touch. • Transfer the muffin tin to a wire rack. Let cool completely before removing the cupcakes. • Prepare a small paper piping bag: Cut a piece of parchment paper into an 8 x 12 x 14-inch (20 x 30 x 35-cm) triangle. Curl the paper into a cone-shape, forming the cone's point mid way along the long side. Tighten the cone and tuck the top flap inside the cone, securing with tape. • **Butter Frosting:** Beat the butter and vanilla in a small bowl using an electric mixer until creamy. • Gradually add the confectioners' sugar until combined. • Divide the frosting between two small bowls. Add the cocoa to one bowl to create a chocolate frosting. • **To Decorate:** Spoon the melted milk chocolate into the prepared piping bag and cut the tip off using scissors or a sharp knife. • Pipe a soccer ball pattern on top of each cupcake. Fill in the gaps with alternate chocolate and vanilla buttercream, using a small spatula or spoon to create a checkered pattern. Pipe over again with chocolate to make a clearly defined pattern if necessary.

MAKES: 12 PREPARATION: 40 MINUTES COOKING: 20–25 MINUTES LEVEL: 2

CUPCAKES

1½ cups (225 g) all-purpose flour
2 teaspoons baking powder
½ teaspoon ground cinnamon
⅛ teaspoon salt
1 cup (200 g) sugar
2 large eggs

½ teaspoon vanilla extract (essence)
1 cup (250 ml) light (single) cream
⅛ teaspoon pink food coloring
3 tablespoons raspberry preserves (jam)

TO DECORATE

1½ cups (225 g) confectioners' (icing) sugar
2 tablespoons water
3 ounces (90 g) dark chocolate, melted
24 small, colored candy-coated buttons

12 red candy-coated chocolate balls
4 candied (glacé) cherries, sliced
4 ice cream wafers or cookies, cut into 12 triangles

CLOWN CUPCAKES

Preheat the oven to 350°F (180°C/gas 4).
• Line a standard 12-cup muffin tin with paper liners. • **Cupcakes:** Combine the flour, baking powder, cinnamon, and salt in a small bowl.
• Beat the sugar, eggs, and vanilla in a medium bowl with an electric mixer on medium-high speed until pale and creamy. • With mixer on low speed, add the mixed dry ingredients, alternating with the cream. • Divide the mixture evenly between two bowls. Stir a few drops of pink food coloring into one bowl, to create a pink batter. • Spoon the batters alternately into the prepared cups, filling each one three-quarters full. • Put a small amount of preserves on top of each cupcake. Create a swirl pattern through the batter using a skewer.
• Bake for 20–25 minutes, until golden brown and firm to the touch. • Transfer the muffin tin to a wire rack. Let cool completely before removing the cupcakes. • Prepare a small paper piping bag: Cut a piece of parchment paper into an 8 x 12 x 14-inch (20 x 30 x 35-cm) triangle. Curl the paper into a cone-shape, forming the cone's point mid way along the long side. Tighten the cone and tuck the top flap inside the cone, securing with tape. • **To Decorate:** combine the confectioners' sugar and water in a small bowl, stirring until smooth. Spread over each cupcake. Before it sets, create a face using 2 colored candy-coated buttons for eyes, a red candy-coated ball for the nose, and a slice of cherry for the mouth. • Spoon the melted chocolate into the prepared piping bag and cut the tip off using scissors or a sharp knife. Pipe "clown-like" shapes around the eyes. Decorate the wafer triangles with the remaining chocolate, piping diagonal stripes. Put the wafers on top of the cupcakes as the clowns' hats, securing with a little melted chocolate. Refer to photograph.

MAKES: 12 PREPARATION: 45 MINUTES COOKING: 20–25 MINUTES LEVEL: 3

CUPCAKES

½ cup (75 g) all-purpose (plain) flour
½ cup (75 g) self-rising flour
¼ teaspoon baking soda (bicarbonate of soda)
⅛ teaspoon salt
⅓ cup (90 g) unsalted butter, softened
¼ cup (50 g) firmly packed light brown sugar

¼ cup (60 ml) honey
1 large egg
1 teaspoon vanilla extract (essence)
¼ cup (60 ml) milk
12 novelty or confectionery bees, to decorate

HONEY FROSTING

1 cup (250 g) unsalted butter, softened
2 tablespoons honey
1 teaspoon vanilla extract (essence)
3 cups (450 g) confectioners' (icing) sugar

HONEY BEE CUPCAKES

Preheat the oven to 350°F (180°C/gas 4).
• Line a standard 12-cup muffin tin with paper liners. • **Cupcakes:** Combine both flours, baking soda, and salt in a small bowl. • Beat the butter, sugar, honey, egg, and vanilla in a medium bowl with an electric mixer on low speed until combined. • Add the mixed dry ingredients and milk and beat on low speed until well mixed. • Spoon the batter into the prepared cups, filling each one three-quarters full. • Bake for 20–25 minutes, until golden brown and firm to the touch. • Transfer the muffin tin to a wire rack. Let cool completely before removing the cupcakes. • **Honey Frosting:** Beat the butter, honey, and vanilla in a small bowl using an electric mixer until light and fluffy. Add the confectioners' sugar, beating until combined. • Spoon the frosting into a pastry bag fitted with a plain nozzle. Pipe a spiral "bee hive" on top of each cupcake, starting from the outside and working into the center. Place a novelty or confectionary bee on top of each hive.

66 *If you don't have self-rising flour on hand, substitute with the same quantity of all-purpose (plain) flour and ¾ teaspoon of baking powder.*

MAKES: 12 PREPARATION: 35 MINUTES COOKING: 20–25 MINUTES LEVEL: 2

CUPCAKES

- 1 cup (150 g) all-purpose (plain) flour
- 1 teaspoon baking powder
- ¼ teaspoon baking soda (bicarbonate of soda)
- ⅛ teaspoon salt
- ¼ cup (60 g) unsalted butter, softened
- ⅓ cup (90 ml) rice syrup
- 1 large egg
- 1 teaspoon vanilla extract (essence)
- ¼ cup (60 ml) milk
- 2 medium overripe bananas, mashed

TO DECORATE

- ½ cup (125 ml) heavy (double) cream
- 1 tablespoon blue agave syrup
- ½ teaspoon ground cinnamon
- 1 banana, thinly sliced, to decorate

BANANAS IN PAJAMAS CUPCAKES

Preheat the oven to 325°F (170°C/gas 3).
• Line a standard 12-cup muffin tin with paper liners. • **Cupcakes:** Combine the flour, baking powder, baking soda, and salt in a small bowl.
• Beat the butter, rice syrup, egg, and vanilla in a medium bowl with an electric mixer on low speed until combined. • Add the mixed dry ingredients and milk and beat on low speed until well mixed. • Stir the banana in by hand.

• Spoon the batter into the prepared cups, filling each one three-quarters full. • Bake for 25–30 minutes, until golden brown and firm to the touch. • Transfer the muffin tin to a wire rack. Let cool completely before removing the cupcakes. • **To Decorate:** Beat the cream, blue agave, and cinnamon in a small bowl until thickened. • Spread over the cupcakes. Top with the banana slices.

> ❝ *Rice syrup is a natural sweetener made from cooked rice which is fermented to turn the starches in the rice into sugars. Both rice syrup and blue agave can usually be found in natural food stores and from online suppliers.*

MAKES: 12 PREPARATION: 25 MINUTES COOKING: 25–30 MINUTES LEVEL: 1

CUPCAKES

1	cup (150 g) all-purpose (plain) flour
¼	cup (30 g) shredded (desiccated) coconut
1	teaspoon baking powder
⅛	teaspoon salt
⅓	cup (90 g) unsalted butter, softened
½	cup (100 g) sugar

1	teaspoon finely grated lemon zest
2	large eggs
¼	cup (60 ml) fresh or canned passion fruit pulp, strained

TO DECORATE

1½	cups (225 g) confectioners' (icing) sugar
2	tablespoons water
⅛	teaspoon red food coloring
⅛	teaspoon blue food coloring
⅛	teaspoon yellow food coloring
1	tube black frosting

ALPHABET CUPCAKES

Preheat the oven to 350°F (180°C/gas 4). • Line a standard 12-cup muffin tin with paper liners. • **Cupcakes:** Combine the flour, coconut, baking powder, and salt in a small bowl. • Beat the butter, sugar, and lemon zest in a medium bowl with an electric mixer on medium-high speed until pale and creamy. • Add the eggs one at a time, beating until just blended after each addition. • With mixer on low speed, add the mixed dry ingredients and passion fruit pulp. • Spoon the batter into the prepared cups, filling each one three-quarters full. • Bake for 20–25 minutes, until golden brown and firm to the touch. • Transfer the muffin tin to a wire rack. Let cool completely before removing the cupcakes. • **To Decorate:** Combine the confectioners' sugar and water in a small bowl, stirring until smooth. • Divide the frosting evenly among three small bowls. Dye each bowl a different color. • Spread the frostings over the cupcakes, creating four of each color. Add a tip to the black tube frosting and pipe capital letters on top of the cupcakes. Refer to photograph.

66 *These cupcakes are great for children who are just learning to write. They will enjoy helping to decorate the cupcakes.*

MAKES: 12 PREPARATION: 35 MINUTES COOKING: 20–25 MINUTES LEVEL: 2

CUPCAKES

1½ cups (225 g) all-purpose (plain) flour
2 teaspoons baking powder
⅛ teaspoon salt
1 cup (200 g) sugar
2 large eggs

1 teaspoon vanilla extract (essence)
1 cup (250 ml) cream
1½ tablespoons unsweetened cocoa powder, sifted
2 teaspoons milk

TO DECORATE

1½ cups (225 g) confectioners' (icing) sugar
2 tablespoons water
⅛ teaspoon black food coloring

ZEBRA CUPCAKES

Preheat the oven to 350°F (180°C/gas 4).
• Line a standard 12-cup muffin tin with paper liners. • **Cupcakes:** Combine the flour, baking powder, and salt in a small bowl. • Beat the sugar, eggs, and vanilla in a medium bowl with an electric mixer on medium-high speed until pale and creamy. • With mixer on low speed, add the mixed dry ingredients, alternating with the cream. • Divide the mixture evenly between two bowls. • Blend the cocoa and milk and stir into one bowl, to create a chocolate batter. • Spoon the batters alternately into the prepared cups, filling each one three-quarters full. Create a swirl pattern through the batter using a skewer. • Bake for 20–25 minutes, until golden brown and firm to the touch. • Transfer the muffin tin to a wire rack. Let cool completely before removing the cupcakes. • Prepare two small paper piping bags: Cut a piece of parchment paper into an 8 x 12 x 14-inch (20 x 30 x 35-cm) triangle. Curl the paper into a cone-shape, forming the cone's point mid way along the long side. Tighten the cone and tuck the top flap inside the cone, securing with tape. Repeat to make a second bag. • **To Decorate:** Combine the confectioners' sugar and water in a small bowl, stirring until smooth. Divide evenly between two small bowls. Add a few drops of black food coloring to one to create a black frosting. • Spoon the black and white frostings into separate piping bags and cut the tips off, using scissors or a sharp knife. • Pipe alternate black and white stripes on top of the cupcakes.

MAKES: 12 PREPARATION: 45 MINUTES COOKING: 20–25 MINUTES LEVEL: 2

CUPCAKES

1½	cups (225 g) all-purpose (plain) flour	2	large eggs
2	teaspoon baking powder	½	teaspoon vanilla extract (essence)
⅛	teaspoon salt	1	teaspoon finely grated lemon zest
1	cup (200 g) sugar	1	cup (250 ml) light (single) cream

LEMON BUTTER FROSTING

½	cup (125 g) unsalted butter, softened
1	teaspoon finely grated lemon zest
1½	cups (225 g) confectioners' (icing) sugar

TO DECORATE

Jelly beans

JELLYBEAN CUPCAKES

Preheat the oven to 350°F (180°C/gas 4).
• Line a standard 12-cup muffin tin with paper liners. • **Cupcakes:** Combine the flour, baking powder, and salt in a small bowl. • Beat the sugar, eggs, vanilla, and lemon zest in a medium bowl with an electric mixer on medium-high speed until pale and creamy.
• With mixer on low speed, add the mixed dry ingredients, alternating with the cream.
• Spoon the batter into the prepared cups, filling each one three-quarters full. • Bake for 20–25 minutes, until golden brown and firm to the touch. • Transfer the muffin tin to a wire rack. Let cool completely before removing the cupcakes. • **Lemon Butter Frosting:** Beat the butter and lemon zest in a small bowl using an electric mixer until creamy. Gradually add the confectioners' sugar, beating until combined.
• Spread the frosting over the cupcakes.
• **To Decorate:** Arrange jelly beans around the outside edge of the cupcakes.

CUPCAKES

2	cups (250 g) pecans, ground
1¼	cups (250 g) sugar
¼	cup (30 g) unsweetened cocoa powder, sifted
1	teaspoon baking powder
1	teaspoon ground cinnamon
⅛	teaspoon salt

4	large eggs, lightly beaten
½	cup (125 g) unsalted butter, melted
1	teaspoon vanilla extract (essence)
1	teaspoon finely grated orange zest

BUTTER FROSTING

½	cup (125 g) butter, softened
½	teaspoon vanilla extract (essence)
1½	cups (225 g), plus ⅔ cup (100 g) confectioners' (icing) sugar
⅛	teaspoon red food coloring
1	tablespoon water

TOADSTOOL CUPCAKES

Preheat the oven to 325°F (170°C/gas 3). • Line a standard 12-cup muffin tin with paper liners. • **Cupcakes:** Combine the ground pecans, sugar, cocoa, baking powder, cinnamon, and salt in a medium bowl. • Combine the eggs, butter, vanilla, and orange zest in a small bowl. • Pour the egg mixture into the mixed dry ingredients and stir until combined. • Spoon the batter into the prepared cups, filling each one three-quarters full. • Bake for 30–35 minutes, until golden brown and firm to the touch. • Transfer the muffin tin to a wire rack. Let cool completely before removing the cupcakes. • Prepare a small paper piping bag: Cut a piece of parchment paper into an 8 x 12 x 14-inch (20 x 30 x 35-cm) triangle. Curl the paper into a cone-shape, forming the cone's point mid way along the long side. Tighten the cone and tuck the top flap inside the cone, securing with tape. • **Butter Frosting:** Beat the butter and vanilla in a small bowl using an electric mixer, until creamy. Gradually add the 1½ cups (225 g) of confectioners' sugar, beating until combined. Add the red food coloring to create red frosting. • Spread the frosting over the cupcakes. • Combine the remaining confectioners' sugar and water in a small bowl, stirring until smooth. • Spoon the frosting into the prepared bag and cut the tip off using scissors or a sharp knife. • Pipe white circles on top of each cupcake to resemble a toadstool.

CUPCAKES

- 1 cup (150 g) all-purpose (plain) flour
- ½ cup (100 g) sugar
- 1 teaspoon baking powder
- ¼ teaspoon baking soda (bicarbonate soda)
- ⅛ teaspoon salt
- ⅓ cup (90 g) unsalted butter, softened
- 1 large egg
- ¼ cup (60 ml) milk
- 1 teaspoon vanilla extract (essence)

TO DECORATE

- 1½ cups (225 g) confectioners' (icing) sugar
- 2 tablespoons water
- ⅛ teaspoon blue food coloring
- ⅛ teaspoon yellow food coloring
- 1 tube red frosting

SUPERMAN CUPCAKES

Preheat the oven to 350°F (180°C/gas 4).
• Line a standard 12-cup muffin tin with paper liners. • **Cupcakes:** Combine the flour, sugar, baking powder, baking soda, and salt in a small bowl. • Beat the butter, egg, milk, and vanilla in a medium bowl with an electric mixer on low speed until combined. • Add the mixed dry ingredients and beat on low speed until well combined. • Spoon the batter into the prepared cups, filling each one three-quarters full. • Bake for 20–25 minutes, until golden brown and firm to the touch. • Transfer the muffin tin to a wire rack. Let cool completely before removing the cupcakes. • **To Decorate:** Combine the confectioners' sugar and water in a small bowl, stirring until smooth. Place one-third of the frosting into a separate bowl and add yellow food coloring to create a bright yellow frosting. Add a few drops of blue food coloring to the remaining frosting to create a bright blue frosting. • Spread the blue frosting over the cup cakes. Let set. • Spread the yellow frosting on top of the blue frosting in the superman triangle shape. • Add a tip to the tube of red frosting and pipe a border around the yellow frosting. Then pipe the superman **S** symbol inside. Refer to photograph.

CUPCAKES

- 1½ cups (225 g) all-purpose (plain) flour
- 2 teaspoons baking powder
- ⅛ teaspoon salt
- 1 cup (200 g) sugar
- 2 large eggs
- 2 tablespoons rose water
- 1 cup (250 ml) light (single) cream

BUTTER FROSTING

- ½ cup (125 g) unsalted butter, softened
- ½ teaspoon vanilla extract (essence)
- 1½ cups (225 g) confectioners' (icing) sugar
- ⅛ teaspoon pink food coloring

TO DECORATE

- 24 small, colored candy-coated buttons
- 24 confectionery milk bottles, cut into ear shapes
- Black liquorice
- 12 confectionery teeth

BUNNY RABBIT CUPCAKES

Preheat the oven to 350°F (180°C/gas 4).
• Line a standard 12-cup muffin tin with paper liners. • **Cupcakes:** Combine the flour, baking powder, and salt in a small bowl. • Beat the sugar, eggs, and rose water in a medium bowl with an electric mixer on medium-high speed until pale and creamy. • With mixer on low speed, add the mixed dry ingredients and cream, beating until combined. • Spoon the batter into the prepared cups, filling each one three-quarters full. • Bake for 20–25 minutes, until golden brown and firm to the touch.
• Transfer the muffin tin to a wire rack. Let cool completely before removing the cupcakes.
• **Butter Frosting:** Beat the butter and vanilla in a small bowl using an electric mixer until creamy. Gradually add the confectioners' sugar until combined. • Tinge the frosting pink with food coloring and spread over the cupcakes.
• **To Decorate:** Create a rabbit face using 2 colored candy-coated buttons for eyes, milk bottle cut outs for the ears and a piece of liquorice for the nose. Cut two teeth out of each confectionery set and place where the mouth would be. Finally, cut thin strips of liquorice for the whiskers. Refer to photograph.

66 *If you can't find the confectionary milk bottles for the ears, substitute with almond halves. You may also use almonds to make* **the bunny rabbits' teeth**.

MAKES: 12 PREPARATION: 40 MINUTES COOKING: 20–25 MINUTES LEVEL: 3

CUPCAKES

1¼ cups (180 g) all-purpose (plain) flour
1 teaspoon baking powder
1 teaspoon ground cinnamon
⅛ teaspoon salt
½ cup (125 g) unsalted butter, softened
¾ cup (150 g) sugar
½ teaspoon vanilla extract (essence)
2 large eggs
⅓ cup (90 ml) milk
1 cup (150 g) fresh or frozen (thawed) raspberries
12 flat bottom ice cream cone cups

BUTTER FROSTING

½ cup (125 g) unsalted butter, softened
½ teaspoon vanilla extract (essence)
1½ cups (225 g) confectioners' (icing) sugar
⅛ teaspoon pink food coloring
1 tablespoon unsweetened cocoa powder, sifted

ICE CREAM CONE CUPCAKES

Preheat the oven to 350°F (180°C/gas 4). • Line a standard 12-cup muffin tin with paper liners. • **Cupcakes:** Combine the flour, baking powder, cinnamon, and salt in a small bowl. • Beat the butter, sugar, and vanilla in a medium bowl with an electric mixer on medium-high speed until pale and creamy. • Add the eggs one at a time, beating until just blended after each addition. • With mixer on low speed, add the mixed dry ingredients, alternating with the milk. • Stir the raspberries in by hand. • Spoon the batter into the prepared cups, filling each one three-quarters full. • Bake for 20–25 minutes, until golden brown and firm to the touch. • Transfer the muffin tin to a wire rack. Let cool completely before removing the cupcakes. • Remove the paper cases from the cupcakes. Shape the bottoms of the cakes with a serrated knife so they sit inside the ice cream cones. Place the cupcakes in the cones. • **Butter Frosting:** Beat the butter and vanilla in a small bowl using an electric mixer until creamy. Gradually add the confectioners' sugar until combined. • Divide the buttercream evenly among three small bowls. Add the pink food coloring to one, stir the cocoa powder into another, and leave the other one plain. • Spread the frostings over the cupcakes, creating four of each color.

CUPCAKES

2	cups (300 g) all-purpose (plain) flour
⅓	cup (50 g) unsweetened cocoa powder, sifted
2	teaspoons baking powder
1	teaspoon baking soda (bicarbonate of soda)

⅛	teaspoon salt
½	cup (125 g) unsalted butter, melted
1	cup (250 ml) blue agave
1	cup (250 ml) milk
1½	teaspoons vanilla extract (essence)

FILLING

½	cup (125 ml) heavy (double) cream
1	teaspoon blue agave
½	teaspoon vanilla extract (essence)
¼	teaspoon ground cinnamon

½	cup (60 g) fresh raspberries
½	cup (60 g) fresh strawberries, chopped
½	cup (60 g) fresh blueberries
	Unsweetened cocoa powder, to dust

CHOCOLATE BERRY CREAMS CUPCAKES

Preheat the oven to 350°F (180°C/gas 4).
• Line two standard 12-cup muffin tins with 16 paper liners. • **Cupcakes:** Combine the flour, cocoa, baking powder, baking soda, and salt in a medium bowl. • Combine the butter, blue agave, milk, and vanilla in a medium bowl.
• Pour the blue agave mixture into the mixed dry ingredients and stir until combined. Do not over mix. • Spoon the batter into the prepared cups, filling each one three-quarters full. • Bake for 15–20 minutes, until golden brown and firm to the touch. • Transfer the muffin tin to a wire rack. Let cool completely before removing the cupcakes. • **Filling:** Whip the cream, blue agave, vanilla, and cinnamon in a small bowl using an electric mixer on medium speed until soft peaks form. Stir in the berries. • Cut a small circle about ½ inch (1 cm) deep from the top of each cupcake. Spoon the berry cream inside. Sit the cupcake lids on top and dust with cocoa.

" Chocolate goes beautifully with berry fruit, as these cupcakes will confirm. With no egg or sugar, these are a healthy choice for children with food allergies.

MAKES: 16 PREPARATION: 20 MINUTES COOKING: 15–20 MINUTES LEVEL: 1

CUPCAKES

¾ cup (125 g) all-purpose (plain) flour

3 tablespoons unsweetened cocoa powder, sifted

⅛ teaspoon salt

½ cup (125 g) unsalted butter, softened

¾ cup (150 g) firmly packed dark brown sugar

½ teaspoon vanilla extract (essence)

2 large eggs

3 tablespoons milk

3½ ounces (100 g) marshmallows, chopped

TO DECORATE

1½ cups (225 g) confectioners' (icing) sugar

2½ tablespoons water

½ teaspoon vanilla extract (essence)

½ tablespoon unsweetened cocoa powder, sifted

⅛ teaspoons pink food coloring

24 small, colored candy-coated buttons

Black and red strap liquorice

Cotton candy (candy floss)

Candied (glacé) cherries

FUNNY FACE CUPCAKES

Preheat the oven to 350°F (180°C/gas 4).
• Line a standard 12-cup muffin tin with paper liners. • **Cupcakes:** Combine the flour, cocoa, baking powder, and salt in a small bowl. • Beat the butter, sugar, and vanilla in a medium bowl with an electric mixer on medium-high speed until creamy. • Add the eggs one at a time, beating until just blended after each addition. • With mixer on low speed, add the mixed dry ingredients, alternating with the milk. • Stir the marshmallows in by hand. • Spoon the batter into the prepared cups, filling each one three-quarters full. • Bake for 20–25 minutes, until golden brown and firm to the touch. • Transfer the muffin tin to a wire rack. Let cool completely before removing the cupcakes.
• **To Decorate:** Combine the confectioners' sugar, water, and vanilla in a small bowl, stirring until smooth. • Divide the frosting evenly between two small bowls. Add the cocoa to one and tint the other one light pink with a few drops of food coloring. • Spread the frostings over the cupcakes, making six of each color. • Create funny faces using colored candied buttons for eyes, liquorice and cotton candy for hair, and cherries and liquorice cut-outs for mouths. Get creative and have fun! Refer to photograph for ideas.

CUPCAKES

1   cup (150 g) all-purpose (plain) flour
⅓   cup (50 g) shredded (desiccated) coconut
1½ teaspoons baking powder
⅛   teaspoon salt
½   cup (125 g) unsalted butter, softened
1   cup (200 g) firmly packed light brown sugar

½   teaspoon vanilla extract (essence)
2   large eggs
½   cup (125 ml) milk
½   cup (90 g) milk chocolate chips
12   large pink marshmallows, to decorate

BUTTER FROSTING

½   cup (125 g) unsalted butter, softened
½   teaspoon vanilla extract (essence)
1½ cups (225 g) confectioners' (icing) sugar
⅛   teaspoon pink food coloring
1   ounce (30 g) dark chocolate, melted

184

PIGLET CUPCAKES

Preheat the oven to 350°F (180°C/gas 4).
• Line a standard 12-cup muffin tin with paper liners. • **Cupcakes:** Combine the flour, coconut, baking powder, and salt in a small bowl. • Beat the butter, sugar, and vanilla in a medium bowl with an electric mixer on medium-high speed until creamy. • Add the eggs one at a time, beating until just blended after each addition.
• With mixer on low speed, add the mixed dry ingredients, alternating with the milk. • Stir the chocolate chips in by hand. • Spoon the batter into the prepared cups, filling each one three-quarters full. • Bake for 20–25 minutes, until golden brown and firm to the touch. • Transfer the muffin tin to a wire rack. Let cool completely before removing the cupcakes.

• Prepare a small paper piping bag: Cut a piece of parchment paper into an 8 x 12 x 14-inch (20 x 30 x 35-cm) triangle. Curl the paper into a cone-shape, forming the cone's point mid way along the long side. Tighten the cone and tuck the top flap inside the cone, securing with tape.
• **Butter Frosting:** Beat the butter and vanilla in a small bowl using an electric mixer until creamy. • Gradually add the confectioners' sugar until combined. • Tint the frosting pink with food coloring and spread over the cupcakes.
• Place a marshmallow on top of each cupcake for the piglets' noses. • Spoon the melted chocolate into the prepared piping bag and cut off the tip using scissors or a sharp knife. Pipe eyes and nostrils onto the piglets' faces.

CUPCAKES

¾ cup (125 g) all-purpose (plain) flour
3 tablespoons unsweetened cocoa powder, sifted
1 teaspoon baking powder
⅛ teaspoon salt
½ cup (125 g) unsalted butter, softened

¾ cup (150 g) firmly packed dark brown sugar
½ teaspoon vanilla extract (essence)
2 large eggs
3 tablespoons milk
¼ cup (30 g) candied (glacé) red cherries, coarsely chopped

CHOCOLATE GANACHE

4 ounces (120 g) dark chocolate, coarsely chopped
¼ cup (60 ml) light (single) cream

TO DECORATE

2 Flake chocolate bars
Black liquorice
Candied (glacé) cherries

HEDGEHOG CUPCAKES

Preheat the oven to 350°F (180°C/gas 4). • Line a standard 12-cup muffin tin with paper liners. • **Cupcakes:** Combine the flour, cocoa, baking powder, and salt in a small bowl. • Beat the butter, sugar, and vanilla in a medium bowl with an electric mixer on medium-high speed until creamy. • Add the eggs one at a time, beating until just blended after each addition. • With mixer on low speed, add the mixed dry ingredients alternating with the milk. • Stir the cherries in by hand. • Spoon the batter into the prepared cups, filling each one three-quarters full. • Bake for 20–25 minutes, until risen and firm to the touch. • Transfer the muffin tin to a wire rack. Let cool completely before removing the cupcakes. • **Chocolate Ganache:** Melt the chocolate and cream in a double boiler over barely simmering water, stirring until smooth. Remove from the heat and let cool and thicken. • Spread over the top of each cupcake. • **To Decorate:** Stick broken pieces of Flake bar on top of each cupcake, to resemble hedgehog spikes, leaving a little space for the face. Cut small pieces of liquorice to use for the nose and the eyes and a sliver of cherry for the mouth.

These cupcakes are decorated with the flaky chocolate from Flake bars. If preferred, replace with shards of milk chocolate. Make the shards by melting the chocolate and pouring onto a cold surface. Let set, then cut into long, shard-shaped pieces.

MAKES: 12 PREPARATION: 45 MINUTES COOKING: 20–25 MINUTES LEVEL: 3

CUPCAKES

1	cup (150 g) all-purpose (plain) flour
1	teaspoon baking powder
½	cup (100 g) firmly packed dark brown sugar
1	teaspoon ground cinnamon
¼	teaspoon baking soda (bicarbonate of soda)
⅛	teaspoon salt
⅓	cup (90 g) unsalted butter, softened
1	large egg
¼	cup (60 ml) milk
1	teaspoon vanilla extract (essence)

BUTTER FROSTING

½	cup (125 g) unsalted butter, softened
½	teaspoon vanilla extract (essence)
1½	cups (225 g) confectioners' (icing) sugar

TO DECORATE

	Black strap liquorice
3	ounces (90 g) white chocolate, melted

PIRATE CUPCAKES

Preheat the oven to 350°F (180°C/gas 4).
• Line a standard 12-cup muffin tin with paper liners. • **Cupcakes:** Combine the flour, baking powder, sugar, cinnamon, baking soda, and salt in a small bowl. • Beat the butter, egg, milk, and vanilla in a medium bowl with an electric mixer on low speed until combined. • Add the mixed dry ingredients and beat on low speed until well combined. • Spoon the batter into the prepared cups, filling each one three-quarters full. • Bake for 20–25 minutes, until golden brown and firm to the touch. • Transfer the muffin tin to a wire rack. Let cool completely before removing the cupcakes.
• Prepare a small paper piping bag: Cut a piece of parchment paper into an 8 x 12 x 14-inch

(20 x 30 x 35-cm) triangle. Curl the paper into a cone-shape, forming the cone's point mid way along the long side. Tighten the cone and tuck the top flap inside the cone, securing with tape. • **Butter Frosting:** Beat the butter and vanilla in a small bowl using an electric mixer until creamy. Gradually add the confectioners' sugar, beating until combined. • Spread the frosting over the cupcakes. • **To Decorate:** Cut eye-patch shapes out of the liquorice and thin strips to use as straps. Arrange eye patches on top of the cupcakes as if covering up an eye.
• Spoon the melted chocolate into the prepared bag and cut off the tip using scissors or a sharp knife. Pipe a skull and crossbones on top of each eye patch.

CUPCAKES

- ¾ cup (125 g) all-purpose (plain) flour
- 3 tablespoons unsweetened cocoa powder, sifted
- 1 teaspoon baking powder
- ⅛ teaspoon salt
- ½ cup (125 g) unsalted butter, softened
- ¾ cup (150 g) firmly packed dark brown sugar
- ½ teaspoon vanilla extract (essence)
- 2 large eggs
- 3 tablespoons milk
- ⅓ cup (90 g) raspberry preserves (jam)

CHOCOLATE BUTTERCREAM

- 6 ounces (180 g) dark chocolate
- 1 cup (250 g) unsalted butter, softened
- ½ teaspoon vanilla extract (essence)
- 1 tablespoon milk
- 2 cups (300 g) confectioners' (icing) sugar
- ⅓ cup (90 g) raspberry preserves (jam)

VOLCANO CUPCAKES

Preheat the oven to 350°F (180°C/gas 4). • Line a standard 12-cup muffin tin with paper liners. • **Cupcakes:** Combine the flour, cocoa, baking powder, and salt in a small bowl. • Beat the butter, sugar, and vanilla in a medium bowl with an electric mixer on medium-high speed until creamy. • Add the eggs one at a time, beating until just blended after each addition. • With mixer on low speed, add the mixed dry ingredients, alternating with the milk. • Spoon half the batter into the prepared cups. Place some raspberry preserves in the center of each one and spoon the remaining batter over the top, filling each one three-quarters full. • Bake for 20–25 minutes, until risen and firm to the touch. • Transfer the muffin tin to a wire rack. Let cool completely before removing the cupcakes. • **Chocolate Buttercream:** Melt the chocolate in a double boiler over barely simmering water, stirring until smooth. Remove from the heat and let cool. • Beat the butter and vanilla in a medium bowl with an electric mixer on medium-high speed until pale and creamy. • Pour in the milk and cooled chocolate, beating until blended. • Gradually add the confectioners' sugar, beating until blended. • Pile the frosting on top of each cupcake using the back of a spoon or spatula to create a volcano shape. • Make an indent at the top. • Thin down the raspberry preserves with a little hot water. • Spoon the raspberry preserves into the top of each "volcano," allowing it to run down the sides a little.

MAKES: 12 PREPARATION: 40 MINUTES COOKING: 20–25 MINUTES LEVEL: 2

CUPCAKES
1½ cups (225 g) all-purpose (plain) flour
2 teaspoons baking powder
⅛ teaspoon salt
1 cup (200 g) sugar
2 large eggs
1 teaspoon vanilla extract (essence)
1 cup (250 ml) light (single) cream

WHITE CHOCOLATE BUTTERCREAM
3 ounces (90 g) white chocolate
½ cup (125 g) unsalted butter, softened
¼ teaspoon vanilla extract (essence)
½ tablespoon milk
⅛ teaspoon pink food coloring
1 cup (150 g) confectioners' (icing) sugar

TO DECORATE
Persian fairy floss

FAIRY FLOSS CUPCAKES

Preheat the oven to 350°F (180°C/gas 4). • Line a standard 12-cup muffin tin with paper liners. • **Cupcakes:** Combine the flour, baking powder, and salt in a small bowl. • Beat the sugar, eggs, and vanilla in a medium bowl with an electric mixer on medium-high speed until pale and creamy. • With mixer on low speed, add the mixed dry ingredients and cream. • Spoon the batter into the prepared cups, filling each one three-quarters full. • Bake for 20–25 minutes, until golden brown and firm to the touch. • Transfer the muffin tin to a wire rack. Let cool completely before removing the cupcakes. • **White Chocolate Buttercream:** Melt the chocolate in a double boiler over barely simmering water, stirring until smooth. Remove from the heat and let cool. • Beat the butter and vanilla in a medium bowl with an electric mixer on medium-high speed until pale and creamy. • Pour in the milk and cooled chocolate, beating until blended. • Gradually add the confectioners' sugar, beating until blended. • Tint the buttercream pink with food coloring and spoon into a pastry bag fitted with a star shaped nozzle. Pipe a rosette on top of each cupcake and top with Persian fairy floss.

❝ *Persian fairy floss, also known as pashmak, is an Iranian sweet. It is available in many gourmet food stores and from online suppliers. Replace with cotton candy (candy floss), if preferred.*

MAKES: 12 PREPARATION: 35 MINUTES COOKING: 20–25 MINUTES LEVEL: 2

CUPCAKES

1½	cups (225 g) all-purpose (plain) flour
2	teaspoons baking powder
⅛	teaspoon salt
1	cup (200 g) firmly packed light brown sugar

2	large eggs
1	teaspoon vanilla extract (essence)
1	cup (250 ml) light (single) cream
½	cup (50 g) chocolate coated honeycomb, coarsely chopped

TO DECORATE

½	cup (125 ml) heavy (double) cream
1	cup (100 g) chocolate coated honeycomb, coarsely chopped

HOKEY POKEY CUPCAKES

Preheat the oven to 350°F (180°C/gas 4). • Line a standard 12-cup muffin tin with paper liners. • **Cupcakes:** Combine the flour, baking powder, and salt in a small bowl. • Beat the sugar, eggs, and vanilla in a medium bowl with an electric mixer on medium-high speed until pale and creamy. • With mixer on low speed, add the mixed dry ingredients and cream. • Stir the honeycomb in by hand. • Spoon the batter into the prepared cups, filling each one three-quarters full. • Bake for 20–25 minutes, until golden brown and firm to the touch. • Transfer the muffin tin to a wire rack. Let cool completely before removing the cupcakes. • Whip the cream in a small bowl using an electric mixer on medium speed until soft peaks form. • Stir the honeycomb into the cream and spoon on top of each cupcake.

66 *The honeycomb chocolate adds a delicious crunch to these cupcakes.*

MAKES: 12 PREPARATION: 30 MINUTES COOKING: 20–25 MINUTES LEVEL: 1

CUPCAKES

1⅓	cups (200 g) all-purpose (plain) flour
1½	teaspoons baking powder
⅛	teaspoon salt
½	cup (125 g) unsalted butter, softened
1	cup (200 g) firmly packed light brown sugar
1	teaspoon vanilla extract (essence)
2	large eggs
½	cup (125 ml) milk

MERINGUE TOPPING

¾	cup (150 g) superfine (caster) sugar
2	large egg whites
	Blue colored sugar crystals, to decorate

WIPE OUT CUPCAKES

Preheat the oven to 350°F (180°C/gas 4).
• Line a standard 12-cup muffin tin with paper liners. • **Cupcakes:** Combine the flour, baking powder, and salt into a small bowl. • Beat the butter, sugar, and vanilla in a medium bowl with an electric mixer on medium-high speed, until creamy. • Add the eggs one at a time, beating until just blended after each addition. • With mixer on low speed, add the mixed dry ingredients and milk. • Spoon the batter into the prepared cups, filling each one three-quarters full. • Bake for 20–25 minutes, until golden brown and firm to the touch. • Transfer the muffin tin to a wire rack. Let cool completely before removing the cupcakes.
• **Meringue Topping:** Place the sugar and egg whites in a heat proof bowl over a saucepan of simmering water. Whisk the mixture until it is thick and glossy, about 5 minutes. • Spoon the meringue on top of the cupcakes. Using a spatula or the back of a spoon create a wave like peak. Sprinkle with blue sugar crystals.

" Young surfers will love these. If the egg whites are brought to a temperature of 160°F (80°C), they are safe to consume in this unbaked meringue topping.

MAKES: 12 PREPARATION: 30 MINUTES COOKING: 25–30 MINUTES LEVEL: 2

CUPCAKES

¾ cup (125 g) all-purpose (plain) flour

3 tablespoons unsweetened cocoa powder, sifted

1 teaspoon baking powder

⅛ teaspoon salt

½ cup (125 g) unsalted butter, softened

¾ cup (150 g) firmly packed dark brown sugar

½ teaspoon vanilla extract (essence)

2 large eggs

3 tablespoons milk

½ cup (90 g) butterscotch chips

TO DECORATE

1½ cups (225 g) confectioners' (icing) sugar

2 tablespoons water

⅛ teaspoon black food coloring

12 confectionery racing cars

RACING CAR CUPCAKES

Preheat the oven to 350°F (180°C/gas 4). • Line a standard 12-cup muffin tin with paper liners. • **Cupcakes:** Combine the flour, cocoa, baking powder, and salt in a small bowl. • Beat the butter, sugar, and vanilla in a medium bowl with an electric mixer on medium-high speed until creamy. • Add the eggs one at a time, beating until just blended after each addition. • With mixer on low speed, add the mixed dry ingredients and milk. • Stir the chocolate chips in by hand. • Spoon the batter into the prepared cups, filling each one three-quarters full. • Bake for 20–25 minutes, until golden brown and firm to the touch. • Transfer the muffin tin to a wire rack. Let cool completely before removing the cupcakes. • **To Decorate:** Combine the confectioners' sugar and water in a small bowl, stirring until smooth. Add a few drops of black food coloring to create a black frosting. • Spread over the tops of the cupcakes and place a racing car on top.

66 *If you can't find butterscotch chips, replace with standard dark or milk chocolate chips.*

MAKES: 12 PREPARATION: 30 MINUTES COOKING: 20–25 MINUTES LEVEL: 2

CUPCAKES

½ cup (75 g) whole-wheat (wholemeal) flour

1 cup (100 g) ground almonds

1 teaspoon baking powder

½ cup (125 g) firmly packed light brown sugar

2 large eggs

2 teaspoons finely grated orange zest

½ cup (125 ml) freshly squeezed orange juice, strained

CREAM CHEESE FROSTING

⅓ cup (90 g) low-fat cream cheese, softened

½ teaspoon finely grated orange zest

⅓ cup (50 g) confectioners' (icing) sugar

¼ cup (60 ml) freshly squeezed orange juice, strained

1 teaspoon freshly squeezed orange juice, strained

1½ ounces (45 g) dark chocolate, melted

ORANGE SWIRLS CUPCAKES

Preheat the oven to 350°F (180°C/gas 4). • Line a standard 12-cup muffin tin with paper liners. • **Cupcakes:** Combine the flour, almonds, and baking powder in a small bowl. • Beat the brown sugar, eggs, and orange zest in a medium bowl with an electric mixer on medium-high speed until creamy. • With mixer on low speed, add the mixed dry ingredients, alternating with the orange juice. • Spoon the batter into the prepared cups, filling each one three-quarters full. • Bake for 20–25 minutes, until golden brown and firm to the touch. • Transfer the muffin tin to a wire rack. Let cool completely before removing the cupcakes. • Prepare a small paper piping bag: Cut a piece of parchment paper into an 8 x 12 x 14-inch (20 x 30 x 35-cm) triangle. Curl the paper into a cone-shape, forming the cone's point mid way along the long side. Tighten the cone and tuck the top flap inside the cone, securing with tape. • **Cream Cheese Frosting:** Beat the cream cheese and orange zest in a small bowl using an electric mixer until creamy. Add the confectioners' sugar and orange juice, beating until combined. • Spread the frosting on the cupcakes. • Spoon the melted chocolate into the prepared piping bag and cut off the tip using scissors or a sharp knife. • Pipe a swirl pattern on top of each cupcake, starting from the center and working to the outside.

MAKES: 12 PREPARATION: 35 MINUTES COOKING: 20–25 MINUTES LEVEL: 2

CUPCAKES

1½	cups (225 g) all-purpose (plain) flour
2	tablespoons unsweetened cocoa powder, sifted
1½	teaspoons baking powder
⅛	teaspoon salt
1	cup (200 g) sugar
2	large eggs
1	teaspoon vanilla extract (essence)
1	cup (250 ml) heavy (double) cream
½	cup (90 g) milk chocolate chips

BUTTER FROSTING

½	cup (125 g) unsalted butter, softened
½	teaspoon vanilla extract (essence)
1½	cups (225 g) confectioners' (icing) sugar
⅛	teaspoon orange food coloring

TO DECORATE

24	small, colored candy-coated buttons
	Black liquorice
	Red liquorice

TABBY CAT CUPCAKES

Preheat the oven to 350°F (180°C/gas 4).
• Line a standard 12-cup muffin tin with paper liners. • **Cupcakes:** Combine the flour, cocoa, baking powder, and salt in a small bowl. • Beat the sugar, eggs, and vanilla in a medium bowl with an electric mixer on medium-high speed until pale and creamy. • With mixer on low speed, add the mixed dry ingredients, alternating with the cream. • Stir in the chocolate chips by hand. • Spoon the batter into the prepared cups, filling each one three-quarters full. • Bake for 20–25 minutes, until golden brown and firm to the touch. • Transfer the muffin tin to a wire rack. Let cool completely before removing the cupcakes.

• **Butter Frosting:** Beat the butter and vanilla in a small bowl using an electric mixer until creamy. Gradually add the confectioners' sugar until combined. • Divide the frosting evenly between two small bowls. Tint one bowl with orange food coloring. • **To Decorate:** Roughly spread the two butter creams on top of the cupcakes to create mottled tabby cat-type markings. • Create cat faces using candy-coated buttons for eyes and small triangles of black liquorice for the nose. Slice thin strips of black liquorice and use for whiskers. Finally, cut thin strips of red liquorice for mouths and small pieces for tongues. Refer to photograph.

MAKES: 12 PREPARATION: 45 MINUTES COOKING: 20–25 MINUTES LEVEL: 2

party
cupcakes

CUPCAKES

3 ounces (90 g) dark chocolate, coarsely chopped
½ cup (125 ml) freshly squeezed orange juice, strained
⅔ cup (100 g) all-purpose (plain) flour
½ cup (50 g) ground almonds
2 tablespoons unsweetened cocoa powder, sifted

1 teaspoon baking powder
⅛ teaspoon salt
⅓ cup (90 g) unsalted butter, softened
1 cup (200 g) firmly packed light brown sugar
1 teaspoon finely grated orange zest
2 large eggs
1 tablespoon orange marmalade

TO DECORATE

1½ cups (225 g) confectioners' (icing) sugar
2 tablespoons water
Black strap liquorice

BAT CUPCAKES

Preheat the oven to 325°F (170°C/gas 3).
• Line a standard 12-cup muffin tin with paper liners. • **Cupcakes:** Melt the chocolate and orange juice in a double boiler over barely simmering water, stirring until smooth. Remove from the heat and let cool. • Combine the flour, almonds, cocoa, baking powder, and salt in a small bowl. • Beat the butter, sugar, and zest in a medium bowl with an electric mixer on medium-high speed until creamy. • Add the eggs one at a time, beating until just blended after each addition. • With mixer on low speed, add the mixed dry ingredients, melted chocolate, and marmalade. • Spoon the batter into the prepared cups, filling each one three-quarters full. • Bake for 25–30 minutes, until risen and firm to the touch. • Transfer the muffin tin to a wire rack. Let cool completely before removing the cupcakes. • **To Decorate:** Using a small shrap knife, cut 12 bat shapes out of the liquorice. • Combine the confectioners' sugar and water in a small bowl, stirring until smooth. • Spread the frosting over the cupcakes and place the bat cut-outs on top.

" These cupcakes are fun to make for a child's birthday party. Children will also enjoy helping you prepare the cupcakes.

MAKES: 12 PREPARATION: 30 MINUTES COOKING: 25–30 MINUTES LEVEL: 2

CUPCAKES

¾	cup (125 g) all-purpose (plain) flour
3	tablespoons unsweetened cocoa powder, sifted
1	teaspoon baking powder
⅛	teaspoon salt
½	cup (125 g) unsalted butter, softened
¾	cup (150 g) firmly packed dark brown sugar
½	teaspoon vanilla extract (essence)
2	large eggs
3	tablespoons milk

TO DECORATE

1½	cups (225 g) confectioners' (icing) sugar
2	tablespoons water
⅛	teaspoon yellow food coloring
12	confectionery black cats

BLACK CAT CUPCAKES

Preheat the oven to 325°F (170°C/gas 3). • Line a standard 12-cup muffin tin with paper liners. • **Cupcakes:** Combine the flour, cocoa, baking powder, and salt in a small bowl. • Beat the butter, sugar, and vanilla in a medium bowl with an electric mixer on medium-high speed until creamy. • Add the eggs one at a time, beating until just blended after each addition. • With mixer on low speed, add the mixed dry ingredients, alternating with the milk. • Spoon the batter into the prepared cups, filling each one three-quarters full. • Bake for 20–25 minutes, until golden brown and firm to the touch. • Transfer the muffin tin to a wire rack. Let cool completely before removing the cupcakes. • **To Decorate:** Combine the confectioners' sugar and water in a small bowl, stirring until smooth. Add yellow food coloring to create a bright yellow frosting. • Spread the frosting over the cupcakes and place black cats on top.

MAKES: 12 PREPARATION: 20 MINUTES COOKING: 20–25 MINUTES LEVEL: 1

CUPCAKES

1⅓ cups (200 g) all-purpose (plain) flour

1½ teaspoons baking powder

⅛ teaspoon salt

½ cup (125 g) unsalted butter, softened

1 cup (200 g) firmly packed light brown sugar

1 teaspoon vanilla extract (essence)

2 large eggs

½ cup (125 ml) milk

TO DECORATE

1½ cups (225 g) confectioners' (icing) sugar

2 tablespoons water

⅛ teaspoon black food coloring

SKULL & CROSSBONES CUPCAKES

Preheat the oven to 350°F (180°C/gas 4). • Line a standard 12-cup muffin tin with paper liners. • **Cupcakes:** Combine the flour, baking powder, and salt in a small bowl. • Beat the butter, sugar, and vanilla in a medium bowl with an electric mixer on medium-high speed until creamy. • Add the eggs one at a time, beating until just blended after each addition. • With mixer on low speed, add the mixed dry ingredients, alternating with the milk. • Spoon the batter into the prepared cups, filling each one three-quarters full. • Bake for 20–25 minutes, until golden brown and firm to the touch. • Transfer the muffin tin to a wire rack. Let cool completely before removing the cupcakes. • Prepare a small paper piping bag: Cut a piece of parchment paper into an 8 x 12 x 14-inch (20 x 30 x 35-cm) triangle. Curl the paper into a cone-shape, forming the cone's point mid way along the long side. Tighten the cone and tuck the top flap inside the cone, securing with tape. • **To Decorate:** Combine the confectioners' sugar and water in a small bowl, stirring until smooth. Transfer a quarter of the mixture to a small bowl. Add black food coloring to the larger portion to create a black frosting. Spread the black frosting over the cupcakes. • Spoon the white frosting into the prepared piping bag and cut the tip off using scissors or a sharp knife. • Pipe a skull and crossbones on to the cupcakes. • Alternatively you can use readymade skull and crossbones confectionery to decorate if available. Refer to photograph.

CUPCAKES

- ¾ cup (125 g) all-purpose (plain) flour
- 1 teaspoon baking powder
- ½ teaspoon ground cinnamon
- ⅛ teaspoon salt
- ½ cup (125 g) unsalted butter, softened
- ¾ cup (150 g) sugar
- ½ teaspoon vanilla extract (essence)
- 2 large eggs
- 3 tablespoons milk
- 3½ ounces (100 g) mini marshmallows

CHOCOLATE GANACHE

- 4 ounces (120 g) dark chocolate, coarsely chopped
- ¼ cup (60 ml) light (single) cream Confectioner's (icing) sugar, to dust

212 SPOOKY CUPCAKES

Preheat the oven to 350°F (180°C/gas 4).
• Line a standard 12-cup muffin tin with paper liners. • **Cupcakes:** Combine the flour, baking powder, cinnamon, and salt in a small bowl.
• Beat the butter, sugar, and vanilla in a medium bowl with an electric mixer on medium-high speed until pale and creamy.
• Add the eggs one at a time, beating until just blended after each addition. • With mixer on low speed, add the mixed dry ingredients, alternating with the milk. • Stir the marshmallows in by hand. • Spoon the batter into the prepared cups, filling each one three-quarters full. • Bake for 20–25 minutes, until golden brown and firm to the touch. • Transfer

the muffin tin to a wire rack. Let cool completely before removing the cupcakes.
• **To Decorate:** Using a small square of thin card or plastic sheet, create a ghost template: Draw the outline of a ghost on the card or plastic and cut out using a sharp knife or scissors.
Chocolate Ganache: Melt the chocolate and cream in a double boiler over barely simmering water, stirring until smooth. Remove from the heat and let cool. • Spread the ganache over the cupcakes and let set. • Place the ghost template over each cupcake and dust with a thick layer of confectioners' sugar to create a ghost design. Refer to the photograph.

CUPCAKES

¾ cup (125 g) all-purpose (plain) flour
1 teaspoon baking powder
1 teaspoon allspice or pumpkin pie spice
⅛ teaspoon salt
½ cup (125 ml) sunflower oil

½ cup (100 g) firmly packed light brown sugar
2 large eggs
1 teaspoon finely grated orange zest
½ cup (120 g) grated butternut squash or pumpkin

TO DECORATE

1½ cups (225 g) confectioners' (icing) sugar
2 tablespoons water
⅛ teaspoon orange food coloring
1 tube black frosting

JACK-O'-LANTERN CUPCAKES

Preheat the oven to 325°F (170°C/gas 3).
• Line a standard 12-cup muffin tin with paper liners. • **Cupcakes:** Combine the flour, baking powder, spice, and salt in a small bowl.
• Combine the oil, sugar, eggs, and zest in a medium bowl. • Stir in the pumpkin and mix in the dry ingredients. • Spoon the batter into the prepared cups, filling each one three-quarters full. • Bake for 25–30 minutes, until golden brown and firm to the touch. • Transfer the muffin tin to a wire rack. Let cool completely before removing the cupcakes. • **To Decorate:** Combine the confectioners' sugar and water in a small bowl, stirring until smooth. • Add orange food coloring to create a bright orange frosting and spread over the cupcakes. • Fit the tube of black frosting with a tip and pipe a Jack-o'-Lantern design on each cupcake. Refer to the photograph.

66 *Jack-o'-Lantern is the hollowed out pumpkin made at Halloween. Prepare these cupcakes at Halloween and give them to children who come trick or treating.*

MAKES: 12 PREPARATION: 30 MINUTES COOKING: 25–30 MINUTES LEVEL: 2

CUPCAKES

1	cup (150 g) all-purpose (plain) flour
½	cup (100 g) firmly packed dark brown sugar
1	teaspoon baking powder
½	teaspoon ground ginger
½	teaspoon ground cinnamon
¼	teaspoon ground nutmeg

¼	teaspoon baking soda (bicarbonate of soda)
⅛	teaspoon salt
⅓	cup (90 g) unsalted butter, softened
1	large egg
¼	cup (60 ml) milk
2	tablespoons candied (glacé) ginger, finely chopped

TO DECORATE

1½	cups (225 g) confectioners' (icing) sugar
2	tablespoons water
12	confectionery mint leaves

CHRISTMAS TREE CUPCAKES

Preheat the oven to 350°F (180°C/gas 4). • Line a standard 12-cup muffin tin with paper liners. • **Cupcakes:** Combine the flour, sugar, baking powder, spices, baking soda, and salt in a medium bowl. • Beat the butter, egg, milk, and ginger in a medium bowl with an electric mixer on low speed until combined. • Add the mixed dry ingredients and beat on low speed until just combined. • Spoon the batter into the prepared cups, filling each one three-quarters full. • Bake for 20–25 minutes, until golden brown and firm to the touch. • Transfer the muffin tin to a wire rack. Let cool completely before removing the cupcakes. • **To Decorate:** Combine the confectioners' sugar and water in a small bowl, stirring until smooth. • Spread the frosting over the cup cakes. • Cut the mint leaves into small slivers and arrange on top of the cupcakes to create a Christmas tree design. Refer to the photograph.

66 These cupcakes are easy and quick to make. Prepare a double batch and freeze half. They can be quickly thawed for unexpected guests at Christmas time.

MAKES: 12 PREPARATION: 25 MINUTES COOKING: 20–25 MINUTES LEVEL: 1

CUPCAKES

3   ounces (90 g) white chocolate, coarsely chopped
⅓   cup (90 ml) light (single) cream
¾   cup (150 g) all-purpose (plain) flour
½   cup (50 g) ground almonds

1   teaspoon baking powder
⅛   teaspoon salt
⅓   cup (90 g) unsalted butter, softened
1   cup (200 g) sugar
1   teaspoon vanilla extract (essence)
2   large eggs

WHITE CHOCOLATE BUTTERCREAM

6   ounces (180 g) white chocolate
½   cup (125 g) unsalted butter, softened
¼   teaspoon vanilla extract (essence)
½   tablespoon milk
1   cup (150 g) confectioners' (icing) sugar

WHITE CHRISTMAS CUPCAKES

Preheat the oven to 325°F (170°C/gas 3).
• Line a standard 12-cup muffin tin with paper liners. • **Cupcakes:** Melt the chocolate and cream in a double boiler over barely simmering water, stirring until smooth. Remove from the heat and let cool. • Combine the flour, almonds, baking powder, and salt in a small bowl. • Beat the butter, sugar, and vanilla in a medium bowl with an electric mixer on medium-high speed until pale and creamy.
• Add the eggs one at a time, beating until just blended after each addition. • With mixer on low speed, add the mixed dry ingredients and melted chocolate. • Spoon the batter into the prepared cups, filling each one three-quarters full. • Bake for 25–30 minutes, until golden brown and firm to the touch. • Transfer the muffin tin to a wire rack. Let cool completely

before removing the cupcakes. • **White Chocolate Buttercream:** Melt half the chocolate in a double boiler over barely simmering water, stirring until smooth. Remove from the heat and let cool. • Beat the butter and vanilla in a medium bowl with an electric mixer on medium-high speed until creamy. • Pour in the milk and cooled chocolate, beating until blended. Gradually add the confectioners' sugar, beating until blended.
• Spread the buttercream on the cupcakes.
• Melt the remaining chocolate in a double boiler over barely simmering water, stirring until smooth. Remove from the heat and let cool. • Pour the chocolate onto a clean glass, marble, or stainless steel surface and allow to set. • Create chocolate curls using a small knife and pile on top of the cupcakes.

CUPCAKES

1⅓	cups (200 g) all-purpose (plain) flour	½	teaspoon peppermint extract (essence)
¼	cup (30 g) shredded (desiccated) coconut	1	cup (250 ml) light (single) cream
1½	teaspoons baking powder	½	cup (90 g) white chocolate chips
⅛	teaspoon salt	12	mini candy canes, to decorate
1	cup (200 g) sugar		
2	large eggs		

BUTTER FROSTING

½	cup (125 g) unsalted butter, softened
½	teaspoon vanilla extract (essence)
1½	cups (225 g) confectioners' (icing) sugar
½	teaspoon peppermint extract (essence)
⅛	teaspoon green food coloring

CANDY CANE CUPCAKES

Preheat the oven to 350°F (180°C/gas 4).
• Line a standard 12-cup muffin tin with paper liners. • **Cupcakes:** Combine the flour, coconut, baking powder, and salt in a small bowl. • Beat the sugar, eggs, and peppermint in a medium bowl with an electric mixer on medium-high speed until pale and creamy. • With mixer on low speed, add the mixed dry ingredients and cream. • Stir in the chocolate chips by hand. • Spoon the batter into the prepared cups, filling each one three-quarters full. • Bake for 20–25 minutes, until golden brown and firm to the touch. • Transfer the muffin tin to a wire rack. Let cool completely before removing the cupcakes. • **Butter Frosting:** Beat the butter and vanilla in a small bowl using an electric mixer until creamy. • Gradually add the confectioners' sugar, beating until combined. Add peppermint extract to flavor. Tint the frosting light green with a few drops of food coloring. • Spread the frosting over the cupcakes and place the candy canes on top.

" *These striking cupcakes are great for many occasions, including birthday parties and St. Patrick's Day.*

MAKES: 12 PREPARATION: 30 MINUTES COOKING: 20–25 MINUTES LEVEL: 2

CUPCAKES

½ cup (90 g) candied (glacé) cherries, chopped
½ cup (90 g) dried figs, finely chopped
½ cup (90 g) raisins
3 tablespoons brandy
1 cup (150 g) all-purpose (plain) flour
1½ teaspoons baking powder

1 teaspoon ground cinnamon
⅛ teaspoon salt
½ cup (125 g) unsalted butter, softened
¾ cup (150 g) firmly packed light brown sugar
2 teaspoons finely grated orange zest
2 large eggs

TO DECORATE

½ cup (75 g) confectioners' (icing) sugar
1 pound (500 g) ready-to-use white fondant
⅓ cup (100 g) orange marmalade, warmed and strained
⅛ teaspoon green food coloring
⅛ teaspoon red food coloring
1 ounce (30 g) white chocolate, melted

CHRISTMAS PUDDING CUPCAKES

Preheat the oven to 375°F (190°C/gas 5). • Line a standard 12-cup muffin tin with paper liners. • **Cupcakes:** Combine the cherries, figs, and raisins in a small bowl. Pour in the brandy and leave to plump for 15 minutes. • Combine the flour, baking powder, cinnamon, and salt into a small bowl. • Beat the butter, sugar, and orange zest in a medium bowl with an electric mixer on medium-high speed until creamy. • Add the eggs one at a time, beating until just blended. • With mixer on low speed, add the mixed dry ingredients and dried fruit. • Spoon the batter into the prepared cups, filling each one three-quarters full. • Bake for 15–20 minutes, until golden brown and firm to the touch. • Transfer the muffin tin to a wire rack. Let cool completely before removing the cupcakes. • **To Decorate:** Dust a clean work surface with confectioners' sugar and knead the fondant until smooth. Roll out to ¼ inch (5 mm) thick. • Using a cookie cutter, cut out rounds big enough to cover the tops of the cupcakes. • Brush the cupcakes with marmalade and place the fondant rounds on top. • Add green food coloring to two-thirds of the remaining fondant and red coloring to the other third. • Roll the green fondant out to ⅛ inch (3 mm) thick. Using a small shape knife cut out twenty-four holly leaves. • Roll the red fondant into twenty-four small red berries. Stick two holly leaves and three berries onto each cupcake, using a little melted chocolate to hold in place.

CUPCAKES

3 ounces (90 g) dark chocolate, coarsely chopped

⅓ cup (90 ml) light (single) cream

⅔ cup (100 g) all-purpose (plain) flour

½ cup (50 g) ground almonds

2 tablespoons unsweetened cocoa powder, sifted

1 teaspoon baking powder

⅛ teaspoon salt

⅓ cup (90 g) unsalted butter, softened

1 cup (200 g) sugar

2 large eggs

WHITE CHOCOLATE BUTTERCREAM

3 ounces (90 g) white chocolate, coarsely chopped

½ cup (125 g) unsalted butter, softened

¼ teaspoon vanilla extract (essence)

½ tablespoon milk

½ cup (75 g) confectioners' (icing) sugar

TO DECORATE

12 milk chocolate Santa Claus

224 SANTA CLAUS CUPCAKES

Preheat the oven to 350°F (180°C/gas 4).
• Line a standard 12-cup muffin tin with paper liners. • **Cupcakes:** Melt the chocolate and cream in a double boiler over barely simmering water, stirring until smooth. Remove from the heat and let cool. • Combine the flour, almonds, cocoa, baking powder, and salt in a small bowl. • Beat the butter and sugar in a medium bowl with an electric mixer on medium-high speed until pale and creamy.
• Add the eggs one at a time, beating until just blended after each addition. • With mixer on low speed, add the mixed dry ingredients and melted chocolate. • Spoon the batter into the prepared cups, filling each one three-quarters full. • Bake for 20–25 minutes, until golden

brown and firm to the touch. • Transfer the muffin tin to a wire rack. Let cool completely before removing the cupcakes. • **White Chocolate Buttercream:** Melt the chocolate in a double boiler over barely simmering water, stirring until smooth. Remove from the heat and let cool. • Beat the butter and vanilla in a medium bowl with an electric mixer on medium-high speed until pale and creamy.
• Pour in the milk and cooled chocolate, beating until blended. Gradually add the confectioners' sugar, beating until blended.
• Spread the buttercream over the cupcakes.
To Decorate: Press a chocolate Santa into the top of each cupcake.

MAKES: 12 PREPARATION: 30 MINUTES COOKING: 20–25 MINUTES LEVEL: 2

CUPCAKES
1½ cups (225 g) all-purpose (plain) flour
1½ teaspoons baking powder
⅛ teaspoon salt
½ cup (125 g) unsalted butter, softened
¾ cup (150 g) sugar
1 teaspoon vanilla extract (essence)
2 large eggs
½ cup (125 ml) milk

TO DECORATE
1½ cups (225 g) confectioners' (icing) sugar
2 tablespoons water
Star-shaped cachous, to decorate
Gold dust, to sprinkle

CHRISTMAS STAR CUPCAKES

Preheat the oven to 350°F (180°C/gas 4).
• Line a standard 12-cup muffin tin with paper liners. • **Cupcakes:** Combine the flour, baking powder, and salt in a small bowl. • Beat the butter, sugar, and vanilla in a medium bowl with an electric mixer on medium-high speed until pale and creamy. • Add the eggs one at a time, beating until just blended after each addition. • With mixer on low speed, add the mixed dry ingredients, alternating with the milk. • Spoon the batter into the prepared cups filling each one three-quarters full. • Bake for 20–25 minutes, until golden brown and firm to the touch. • Transfer the muffin tin to a wire rack. Let cool completely before removing the cupcakes. • **To Decorate:** Combine the confectioners' sugar and water in a small bowl, stirring until smooth. • Spread the frosting over the cupcakes. • Create a star outline on top using the cachous.

66 Cachous are colorful confectionary cake decorations. They come in many sizes and shapes. If you can't find the star-shaped ones mentioned here, cut out stars from colored paper and stick on the cupcakes with a little melted chocolate.

MAKES: 12 PREPARATION: 25 MINUTES COOKING: 20–25 MINUTES LEVEL: 2

CUPCAKES

3 ounces (90 g) dark chocolate

¼ cup (60 g) unsalted butter

½ teaspoon peppermint extract (essence)

1½ cups (225 g) all-purpose (plain) flour

¾ cup (150 g) firmly packed light brown sugar

2 tablespoons unsweetened cocoa powder, sifted

1½ teaspoons baking powder

1 teaspoon baking soda (bicarbonate of soda)

⅛ teaspoon salt

1 cup (250 ml) milk

WHITE MINT GANACHE

4 ounces (120 g) white chocolate, coarsely chopped

¼ cup (60 ml) light (single) cream

¼ teaspoon peppermint extract (essence)

TO DECORATE

2 ounces (60 g) milk chocolate, melted

12 silver balls

CHOCOLATE MINT BUNNY CUPCAKES

EGG FREE

Preheat the oven to 325°F (170°C/gas 3).
• Line a standard 12-cup muffin tin with paper liners. • **Cupcakes:** Melt the chocolate, butter, and peppermint in a double boiler over barely simmering water, stirring until smooth.
• Combine the flour, sugar, cocoa, baking powder, and salt in a medium bowl. • Pour the melted chocolate and milk into the mixed dry ingredients and mix until just combined.
• Spoon the batter into the prepared cups, filling each one three-quarters full. • Bake for 25–30 minutes, until golden brown and firm to the touch. • Transfer the muffin tin to a wire rack. Let cool completely before removing the cupcakes. • Prepare a small paper piping bag:

Cut a piece of parchment paper into an 8 x 12 x 14-inch (20 x 30 x 35-cm) triangle. Curl the paper into a cone-shape, forming the cone's point mid way along the long side. Tighten the cone and tuck the top flap inside the cone, securing with tape. • **White Mint Ganache:** Melt the chocolate and cream in a double boiler over barely simmering water, stirring until smooth. Remove from the heat, stir in the peppermint extract and let cool. • Spread the ganache over the cupcakes. • **To Decorate:** Spoon the melted milk chocolate into the prepared bag and cut the tip off using scissors or a sharp knife. • Pipe rabbit shapes onto the cupcakes and place a silver ball for the tail.

MAKES: 12 PREPARATION: 30 MINUTES COOKING: 25–30 MINUTES LEVEL: 2

CUPCAKES

1½	cups (225 g) all-purpose (plain) flour
3	tablespoons unsweetened cocoa powder, sifted
1½	teaspoons baking powder
⅛	teaspoon salt
1	cup (200 g) sugar
2	large eggs
1	teaspoon vanilla extract (essence)
1	cup (250 ml) cream
½	cup (90 g) milk chocolate chips

CHOCOLATE BUTTERCREAM

3	ounces (90 g) dark chocolate
½	cup (125 g) unsalted butter, softened
¼	teaspoon vanilla extract (essence)
½	tablespoon milk
1	cup (150 g) confectioners' (icing) sugar

TO DECORATE

3	small Flake chocolate bars, crumbled
12	mini speckled Easter eggs
1	ounce (30 g) milk chocolate, melted

EASTER NEST CUPCAKES

Preheat the oven to 350°F (180°C/gas 4).
• Line a standard 12-cup muffin tin with paper liners. • **Cupcakes:** Combine the flour, cocoa, baking powder, and salt in a small bowl. • Beat the sugar, eggs, and vanilla in a medium bowl with an electric mixer on medium-high speed until pale and creamy. • With mixer on low speed, add the mixed dry ingredients and cream. • Stir in the chocolate chips by hand. • Spoon the batter into the prepared cups, filling each one three-quarters full. • Bake for 20–25 minutes, until golden brown and firm to the touch. • Transfer the muffin tin to a wire rack. Let cool completely before removing the cupcakes. • **Chocolate Buttercream:** Melt the chocolate in a double boiler over barely simmering water, stirring until smooth. Remove from the heat and let cool. • Beat the butter and vanilla in a small bowl with an electric mixer on medium-high speed until pale and creamy. • Pour in the milk and cooled chocolate, beating until blended. Gradually add the confectioners' sugar, beating until blended. • Spread the buttercream on the cupcakes. **To Decorate:** Break the flaked chocolate bars into pieces and use to create nests on top of cupcakes. Place speckled eggs in each nest, securing with melted chocolate.

> *These cupcakes are decorated with Flake chocolate bars. If liked, substitute with shards of milk chocolate. Make the shards by melting the chocolate and pouring onto a cold glass or marble surface. Let set, then cut into shard-shaped pieces.*

MAKES: 12 PREPARATION: 30 MINUTES COOKING: 20–25 MINUTES LEVEL: 2

CUPCAKES

1	cup (100 g) all-purpose (plain) flour
1	teaspoon baking powder
½	teaspoon ground cinnamon
½	teaspoon ground nutmeg
¼	teaspoon ground cloves
⅛	teaspoon salt

½	cup (125 g) unsalted butter, softened
¾	cup (150 g) firmly packed light brown sugar
2	large eggs
¼	cup (60 ml) milk
½	cup (90 g) currants
¼	cup (25 g) mixed peel, finely chopped

CINNAMON FROSTING

½	cup (125 g) unsalted butter, softened
2	teaspoons ground cinnamon
1½	cups (225 g) confectioners' sugar

TO DECORATE

½	cup (75 g) confectioners' (icing) sugar
¾	tablespoon water

HOT CROSS BUN CUPCAKES

Preheat the oven to 325°F (170°C/gas 3).
• Line a standard 12-cup muffin tin with paper liners. • **Cupcakes:** Combine the flour, baking powder, cinnamon, nutmeg, cloves, and salt in a small bowl. • Beat the butter and sugar in a medium bowl with an electric mixer on medium-high speed until creamy. • Add the eggs one at a time, beating until just blended after each addition. • With mixer on low speed, add the mixed dry ingredients, alternating with the milk. • Stir in the currants and mixed peel by hand. • Spoon the batter into the prepared cups, filling each one three-quarters full. • Bake for 25–30 minutes, until golden brown and firm to the touch. • Transfer the muffin tin to a wire rack. Let cool completely before removing the cupcakes. • Prepare a small paper piping

bag: Cut a piece of parchment paper into an 8 x 12 x 14-inch (20 x 30 x 35-cm) triangle. Curl the paper into a cone-shape, forming the cone's point mid way along the long side. Tighten the cone and tuck the top flap inside the cone, securing with tape. • **Cinnamon Frosting:** Beat the butter and cinnamon in a small bowl using an electric mixer until creamy. Gradually add the confectioners' sugar, beating until combined. • Spread the frosting over the cupcakes. • **To Decorate:** Combine the confectioners' sugar and water in a small bowl, stirring until smooth. • Spoon the frosting into the prepared piping bag and cut the tip off using scissors or a sharp knife. Pipe a cross on top of each cupcake.

MAKES: 12 PREPARATION: 30 MINUTES COOKING: 25–30 MINUTES LEVEL: 2

CUPCAKES				**TO DECORATE**	
1	cup (150 g) all-purpose (plain) flour	2	teaspoons finely grated orange zest	1½	cups (225 g) confectioners' (icing) sugar
⅓	cup (30 g) ground almonds	2	large eggs	2	tablespoons water
1	teaspoon baking powder	3	tablespoons fresh or canned passion fruit pulp, strained	⅛	teaspoon blue food coloring
⅛	teaspoon salt	2	tablespoons plain yogurt	12	confectionery airplanes
⅓	cup (90 g) unsalted butter, softened				
½	cup (100 g) sugar				

BON VOYAGE CUPCAKES

234

Preheat the oven to 350°F (180°C/gas 4).
• Line a standard 12-cup muffin tin with paper liners. • **Cupcakes:** Combine the flour, almonds, baking powder, and salt in a small bowl.
• Beat the butter, sugar, and orange zest in a medium bowl with an electric mixer on medium-high speed until pale and creamy.
• Add the eggs one at a time, beating until just blended after each addition. • With mixer on low speed, add the mixed dry ingredients, passion fruit pulp, and yogurt. • Spoon the batter into the prepared cups, filling each one three-quarters full. • Bake for 20–25 minutes, until golden brown and firm to the touch.
• Transfer the muffin tin to a wire rack. Let cool completely before removing the cupcakes.
To Decorate: Combine the confectioners' sugar and water in a small bowl, stirring until smooth. Tint the frosting light blue with blue food coloring and spread over the cupcakes.
• Place a confectionery airplane on top of each cupcake.

66 These bright and colorful cupcakes are fun to prepare. Wrap in decorative paper and give to a friend who is planning to travel.

MAKES: 12 PREPARATION: 30 MINUTES COOKING: 20–25 MINUTES LEVEL: 1

CUPCAKES

2	cups (250 g) shredded (desiccated) coconut
6	tablespoons rice flour
⅛	teaspoon salt
4	large eggs
1	cup (200 g) superfine (caster) sugar
3	teaspoons finely grated lime zest

TO DECORATE

2	cups (300 g) confectioners' (icing) sugar
3	tablespoons water
⅛	teaspoon blue food coloring
⅛	teaspoon red food coloring

INDEPENDENCE DAY CUPCAKES

Preheat the oven to 350°F (180°C/gas 4). • Line two standard 12-cup muffin tins with 16 paper liners. • **Cupcakes:** Combine the coconut, rice flour, and salt in a small bowl. • Beat the eggs, sugar, and lime zest in a medium bowl with an electric mixer on medium-high speed until pale and creamy. • Fold in the mixed dry ingredients by hand. • Spoon the batter into the prepared cups, filling each one three-quarters full. • Bake for 20–25 minutes, until golden brown and firm to the touch. • Transfer the muffin tin to a wire rack. Let cool completely before removing the cupcakes. • Prepare three small paper piping bags: Cut a piece of parchment paper into an 8 x 12 x 14-inch (20 x 30 x 35-cm) triangle.

Curl the paper into a cone-shape, forming the cone's point mid way along the long side. Tighten the cone and tuck the top flap inside the cone, securing with tape. Repeat twice to make two more piping bags. • **To Decorate:** Combine the confectioners' sugar and water in a small bowl, stirring until smooth. Divide the frosting evenly among three small bowls. Add blue food coloring to one bowl to create a bright blue frosting. Add red food coloring to another to create a bright red frosting. Spoon the frostings into the prepared piping bags and cut the tips off, using scissors or a sharp knife. Pipe alternate red, white, and blue stripes on the cupcakes.

MAKES: 16 PREPARATION: 30 MINUTES COOKING: 20–25 MINUTES LEVEL: 2

CUPCAKES

1⅓	cups (200 g) all-purpose (plain) flour
1½	teaspoons baking powder
⅛	teaspoon salt
½	cup (125 g) unsalted butter, softened
1	cup (200 g) firmly packed light brown sugar
1	teaspoon vanilla extract (essence)
2	large eggs
½	cup (125 ml) milk

CREAM CHEESE FROSTING

⅔	cup (150 g) cream cheese
½	teaspoon vanilla extract (essence)
⅔	cup (100 g) confectioners' (icing) sugar
1	tablespoon freshly squeezed lemon juice, strained
2	drops green food coloring

TO DECORATE

⅔	cup (100 g) confectioners' (icing) sugar
½	tablespoon water
⅛	teaspoon green food coloring

238 ST. PATRICK'S DAY CUPCAKES

Preheat the oven to 350°F (180°C/gas 4).
• Line a standard 12-cup muffin tin with paper liners. • **Cupcakes:** Combine the flour, baking powder, and salt in a small bowl. • Beat the butter, sugar, and vanilla in a medium bowl with an electric mixer on medium-high speed until creamy. • Add the eggs one at a time, beating until just blended after each addition. • With mixer on low speed, add the mixed dry ingredients, alternating with the milk. • Spoon the batter into the prepared cups, filling each one three-quarters full. • Bake for 20–25 minutes, until golden brown and firm to the touch. • Transfer the muffin tin to a wire rack. Let cool completely before removing the cupcakes. • Prepare a small paper piping bag: Cut a piece of parchment paper into an 8 x 12 x 14-inch (20 x 30 x 35-cm) triangle. Curl the paper into a cone-shape, forming the cone's point mid way along the long side. Tighten the cone and tuck the top flap inside the cone, securing with tape. • **Cream Cheese Frosting:** Beat the cream cheese and vanilla in a small bowl using an electric mixer until creamy. Add the confectioners' sugar and lemon juice, beating until combined. Tint the frosting pale green with the food coloring. • Spread over the cupcakes. • **To Decorate:** Combine the confectioners' sugar and water in a small bowl, stirring until smooth. Add the green food coloring to create a dark green frosting and spoon into the prepared piping bag. Cut the tip off using scissors or a sharp knife and pipe a three leaf clover design on each cupcake.

MAKES: 12 PREPARATION: 45 MINUTES COOKING: 20–25 MINUTES LEVEL: 3

CUPCAKES

- 2 cups (250 g) pecans, ground
- 1¼ cups (250 g) sugar
- ¼ cup (30 g) unsweetened cocoa powder, sifted
- 1 teaspoon baking powder
- 1 teaspoon ground cinnamon
- ⅛ teaspoon salt
- 4 large eggs
- ½ cup (125 ml) melted unsalted butter
- 1 teaspoon vanilla extract (essence)
- 1 teaspoon finely grated orange zest

CHOCOLATE GANACHE

- 4 ounces (120 g) dark chocolate, coarsely chopped
- ¼ cup (60 ml) light (single) cream

TO DECORATE

- 1½ cups (225 g) confectioners' (icing) sugar
- 2 tablespoons water
  Numbered candles

BIRTHDAY CUPCAKES

Preheat the oven to 325°F (170°C/gas 3).
• Line a standard 12-cup muffin tin with paper liners. • **Cupcakes:** Combine the ground pecans, sugar, cocoa, baking powder, cinnamon, and salt in a medium bowl. • Combine the eggs, butter, vanilla, and orange zest in a small bowl.
• Pour the egg mixture into the mixed dry ingredients and stir until just combined.
• Spoon the batter into the prepared cups, filling each one three-quarters full. • Bake for 30–35 minutes, until golden brown and firm to the touch. • Transfer the muffin tin to a wire rack. Let cool completely before removing the cupcakes. • Prepare a small paper piping bag: Cut a piece of parchment paper into an 8 x 12 x 14-inch (20 x 30 x 35-cm) triangle. Curl the

paper into a cone-shape, forming the cone's point mid way along the long side. Tighten the cone and tuck the top flap inside the cone, securing with tape. • **Chocolate Ganache:** Melt the chocolate and cream in a double boiler over barely simmering water, stirring until smooth. Remove from the heat and let cool and thicken. • Spread over the cupcakes.

To Decorate: Combine the confectioners' sugar and water in a small bowl, stirring until smooth. • Spoon into the prepared bag and cut the tip off using scissors or a sharp knife. Pipe a border around the cupcakes and arrange the candles in one cupcake. Pipe the birthday age on the remaining cupcakes.

CUPCAKES

- 1⅓ cups (200 g) all-purpose (plain) flour
- ⅓ cup (30 g) ground almonds
- 1½ teaspoons baking powder
- ½ teaspoons ground cinnamon
- ⅛ teaspoon salt
- 1 cup (200 g) sugar
- 2 large eggs
- 1 teaspoon finely grated orange zest
- 1 teaspoon vanilla extract (essence)
- 1 cup (250 ml) light (single) cream
- 12 milk chocolate squares
- Small cachous, to decorate
- 12 sparklers, to decorate

ORANGE GANACHE

- 4 ounces (120 g) dark chocolate, coarsely chopped
- ¼ cup (60 ml) light (single) cream
- 2 teaspoons finely grated orange zest

HAPPY NEW YEAR CUPCAKES

Preheat the oven to 350°F (180°C/gas 4).
• Line a standard 12-cup muffin tin with silver paper liners. • **Cupcakes:** Combine the flour, almonds, baking powder, cinnamon, and salt in a small bowl. • Beat the sugar, eggs, orange zest, and vanilla in a medium bowl with an electric mixer on medium-high speed until pale and creamy. • With mixer on low speed, add the mixed dry ingredients and cream. • Spoon half the batter into the prepared cups. Place a chocolate square in the center of each one and spoon in the remaining batter, filling each one three-quarters full. • Bake for 20–25 minutes, until golden brown and firm to the touch.
• Transfer the muffin tin to a wire rack. Let cool completely before removing the cupcakes.
Orange Ganache: Melt the chocolate and cream in a double boiler over barely simmering water, stirring until smooth. Remove from the heat, stir in the orange zest, and let cool.
• Spread the ganache over the cupcakes and sprinkle with cachous. • Cut the sparklers down to a shorter size and insert into the cupcakes. Light when ready to serve.

> 66 *These cakes are both tasty and fun to serve. Children will especially love the sparklers.*

MAKES: 12 PREPARATION: 30 MINUTES COOKING: 20–25 MINUTES LEVEL: 2

CUPCAKES

¾ cup (125 g) all-purpose (plain) flour

3 tablespoons unsweetened cocoa powder, sifted

1 teaspoon baking powder

⅛ teaspoon salt

½ cup (125 g) unsalted butter, softened

¾ cup (150 g) firmly packed dark brown sugar

½ teaspoon vanilla extract (essence)

2 large eggs

3 tablespoons milk

3½ ounces (100 g) mini marshmallows, chopped

CHOCOLATE BUTTERCREAM

3 ounces (90 g) dark chocolate

½ cup (125 g) unsalted butter, softened

¼ teaspoon vanilla extract (essence)

½ tablespoon milk

1 cup (150 g) confectioners' (icing) sugar

TO DECORATE

Mini candy-coated chocolate buttons

Colored confectionery sprinkles

12 birthday candles

244 HAPPY BIRTHDAY CUPCAKES

Preheat the oven to 350°F (180°C/gas 4).
• Line a standard 12-cup muffin tin with paper liners. • **Cupcakes:** Combine the flour, cocoa, baking powder, and salt in a small bowl. • Beat the butter, sugar, and vanilla in a medium bowl with an electric mixer on medium-high speed until creamy. • Add the eggs one at a time, beating until just blended after each addition. • With mixer on low speed, add the mixed dry ingredients, alternating with the milk. • Stir the marshmallows in by hand. • Spoon the batter into the prepared cups, filling each one three-quarters full. • Bake for 20–25 minutes, until golden brown and firm to the touch. • Transfer the muffin tin to a wire rack. Let cool completely before removing the cupcakes.

Chocolate Buttercream: Melt the chocolate in a double boiler over barely simmering water, stirring until smooth. Remove from the heat and let cool. • Beat the butter and vanilla in a medium bowl with an electric mixer on medium-high speed until pale and creamy. • Pour in the milk and cooled chocolate, beating until blended. Gradually add the confectioners' sugar, beating until blended. • Spread the buttercream on the cupcakes. • **To Decorate:** Place candy-coated buttons around the outside edge of each cupcake to create a border. Scatter confectionery sprinkles inside the border and arrange the cupcakes on a plate or cake board. • Place a candle in the center of each cupcake and light when ready to serve.

MAKES: 12 PREPARATION: 30 MINUTES COOKING: 20–25 MINUTES LEVEL: 2

special
moments

CUPCAKES

3¼ pounds (1.5 kg) dark chocolate
6 cups (1.5 kg) unsalted butter, chopped
24 large eggs
4 cups (800 g) firmly packed light brown sugar
1 cup (250 ml) maple syrup
4 cups (400 g) ground walnuts
1½ cups (200 g) walnuts, coarsely chopped

ALMOND PRALINE

⅓ cup (70 g) superfine (caster) sugar
1½ tablespoons water
⅓ cup (50 g) flaked almonds

CHOCOLATE GANACHE

1 pound (500 g) dark chocolate, coarsely chopped
1 cup (250 ml) light (single) cream

TO DECORATE

2 ounces (60 g) white chocolate
⅛ teaspoon red food coloring
½ cup (50 g) candied (glacé) ginger, finely chopped
4 ounces (120 g) white chocolate curls

CHOCOLATE DECADENCE CUPCAKES

Preheat the oven to 350°F (180°C/gas 4).
• Line four standard 12-cup muffin tins with 40 paper liners. • **Cupcakes:** Melt the chocolate and butter in a double boiler over barely simmering water, stirring until smooth. Remove from the heat and let cool. • Beat the eggs, sugar, maple syrup, ground walnuts, and chopped walnuts in a large bowl. • Pour in the chocolate and beat until combined. • Spoon the batter into the prepared cups, filling each one three-quarters full. • Bake in batches for 30–35 minutes, until golden brown and firm to the touch. • Transfer the muffin tins to a wire rack. Let cool completely before removing the cupcakes. • **Almond Praline:** Line a baking sheet with parchment paper. • Place the sugar and water in a small pan and gently heat until melted and pale gold, 5–10 minutes. • Stir in the almonds and pour onto the prepared baking sheet. Leave to harden for 20 minutes. • Break the hardened praline into small shards and reserve for decorating.

• Prepare a small paper piping bag: Cut a piece of parchment paper into an 8 x 12 x 14-inch (20 x 30 x 35-cm) triangle. Curl the paper into a cone-shape, forming the cone's point mid way along the long side. Tighten the cone and tuck the top flap inside the cone, securing with tape. • **Chocolate Ganache:** Melt the chocolate and cream in a double boiler over barely simmering water, stirring until smooth. Remove from the heat and let cool. • Spread the ganache over the cupcakes. • **To Decorate:** Melt the white chocolate in a double boiler over barely simmering water, stirring until smooth. Remove from the heat, tint light pink with a few drops of pink food coloring and let cool slightly. • Spoon the pink chocolate into the prepared piping bag and cut the tip off using scissors or a sharp knife. Pipe hearts on top of ten of the cupcakes. • Decorate 10 of the remaining cupcakes with candied ginger, 10 with chocolate curls, and 10 with shards of praline.

MAKES: 40 PREPARATION: 1 HOUR 30 MINUTES COOKING: 1 HOUR LEVEL: 3

CUPCAKES

2	cups (300 g) all-purpose (plain) flour
4	cups (400 g) ground almonds
4	teaspoons baking powder
4	teaspoons ground ginger
2	cups (500 g) firmly packed light brown sugar

8	large eggs
2	tablespoons finely grated orange zest
3	cups (750 ml) freshly squeezed orange juice, strained
4	tablespoons candied (glacé) ginger, finely chopped
1	cup (200 g) sugar

TO DECORATE

1	cup (150 g) confectioners' (icing) sugar
3	pounds (1.5 kg) ready-to-use white fondant
1	cup (325 g) orange marmalade, warmed and strained
1½	teaspoons silver lustre
1½	teaspoons vodka

250

WHITE WEDDING CUPCAKES

Preheat the oven to 350°F (180°C/gas 4). • Line four standard 12-cup muffin tins with silver paper lined baking cups. • **Cupcakes:** Combine the flour, ground almonds, baking powder, and ginger in a small bowl. • Beat the brown sugar, eggs, and orange zest in a large bowl with an electric mixer on medium-high speed until creamy. • With mixer on low speed, add the mixed dry ingredients and ½ cup (125 ml) of the orange juice. • Stir the candied ginger in by hand. • Spoon the batter into the prepared cups, filling each one three-quarters full. • Bake in batches for 20–25 minutes, until golden brown and firm to the touch. • Meanwhile, simmer the remaining orange juice and sugar in a small saucepan over medium-low heat until the sugar has dissolved and the liquid has thickened to a syrup consistency, about 5 minutes. • Pierce the warm cupcakes with a skewer or toothpick several times and brush with the orange syrup. • Transfer the muffin tins to a wire rack. Let cool completely before removing the cupcakes. • **To Decorate:** Dust a clean work surface with confectioners' sugar and knead the fondant until smooth. • Roll out to ¼ inch (5 mm) thick. • Roll over the fondant with a spiral swirl pattern roller. • Using a cookie cutter, cut out rounds large enough to cover the tops of the cupcakes. • Brush the cupcakes with marmalade and place the fondant rounds on top. • Combine the silver lustre and vodka in a small bowl. Using a small paint brush, paint the swirl pattern with lustre and leave to dry.

MAKES: 48 PREPARATION: 1 HOUR 30 MINUTES COOKING: 40–50 MINUTES LEVEL: 3

CUPCAKES

4 cups (600 g) cake flour
1⅓ cups (130 g) ground pistachios
4 teaspoons baking powder
½ teaspoon salt
2 cups (500 g) unsalted butter, softened

4 cups (800 g) sugar
2 teaspoons vanilla extract (essence)
8 large eggs
1⅓ cups (330 ml) milk
⅓ cup (90 ml) rose water

WHITE CHOCOLATE BUTTERCREAM

12 ounces (350 g) white chocolate
2 cups (500 g) unsalted butter, softened
1 teaspoon vanilla extract (essence)
2 tablespoons rose water
4 cups (600 g) confectioners' (icing) sugar

TO DECORATE

Pastel colored sugar flowers

HERE COMES THE BRIDE CUPCAKES

Preheat the oven to 350°F (180°C/gas 4).
• Line four standard 12-cup muffin tins with silver paper liners or pastel-colored baking cups. • **Cupcakes:** Combine the flour, pistachios, baking powder, and salt in a large bowl. • Beat the butter, sugar, and vanilla in a large bowl with an electric mixer on medium-high speed until pale and creamy. • Add the eggs one at a time, beating until just blended after each addition. • With mixer on low speed, add the mixed dry ingredients, milk, and rose water.
• Spoon the batter into the prepared cups, filling each one three-quarters full. • Bake in batches for 20–25 minutes, until golden brown and firm to the touch. • Transfer the muffin tins to wire racks. Let cool completely before removing the cupcakes. • **White Chocolate Buttercream:** Melt the chocolate in a double boiler over barely simmering water, stirring until smooth. Remove from the heat and let cool. • Beat the butter and vanilla in a medium bowl with an electric mixer on medium-high speed until pale and creamy. • Pour in the rose water and cooled chocolate, beating until blended. • Gradually add the confectioners' sugar, beating until blended. • Spoon the buttercream into a pastry bag fitted with a plain nozzle. • Pipe the buttercream onto the cupcakes and decorate with the pastel colored sugar flowers.

MAKES: 48 PREPARATION: 1 HOUR COOKING: 40–50 MINUTES LEVEL: 2

CUPCAKES

2/3 cups (480 g) candied cherries, coarsely chopped
1 1/3 cups (240 g) mixed peel
2 cups (350 g) raisins
1 cup (180 g) currants
1 cup (180 g) dates, coarsely chopped
3/4 cup (120 g) slivered almonds
1/2 cup (125 ml) brandy

2 1/2 cups (375 g) all-purpose (plain) flour
1/2 teaspoon baking soda (bicarbonate of soda)
1 teaspoon pumpkin spice or allspice
1 teaspoon ground cinnamon
1/2 teaspoon ground cloves
1/2 teaspoon salt

1 cup (250 g) unsalted butter, softened
2 cups (400 g) firmly packed light brown sugar
6 large eggs
3/4 cup (180 ml) light molasses
3/4 cup (180 ml) apple juice

TO DECORATE

1 cup (150 g) confectioners' (icing) sugar
4 pounds (2 kg) ready-to-use white fondant
1/8 teaspoon red food coloring
1/8 teaspoon blue food coloring
1 cup (325 g) orange marmalade, warmed and strained
Purple ribbon

HAPPILY EVER AFTER CUPCAKES

Preheat the oven to 275°F (120°C/gas 1). • Line four standard 12-cup muffin tins with 40 paper liners. • **Cupcakes:** Combine the cherries, mixed peel, raisins, currants, dates, and slivered almonds in a medium bowl. Pour the brandy over the fruit and leave to plump overnight. • Stir 1/2 cup (75 g) of the flour into the soaked fruit. • Combine the remaining flour, baking soda, spice, cinnamon, cloves, and salt in a small bowl. • Beat the butter and sugar in a medium bowl with an electric mixer on medium-high speed until pale and creamy. • Add the eggs one at a time, beating until just blended after each addition. • With mixer on low speed, add the mixed dry ingredients, molasses, and apple juice. • Spoon the batter into the prepared cups, filling each one almost full, as the mixture does not rise very much. • Bake in batches for 40–45 minutes, until golden brown and firm to the touch. • Transfer the muffin tins to a wire rack. Let cool completely before removing the cupcakes. **To Decorate:** Dust a clean kitchen work surface with confectioners' sugar. Add the red and blue food coloring to the fondant and knead until smooth and light purple in color. Roll out to 1/4 inch (5 mm) thick. • Use a small sharp knife to cut out rounds that are big enough to entirely cover the cupcakes. • Remove the papers from the cupcakes and brush with marmalade. • Place the fondant rounds on top of the cupcakes. Fold down to envelop the cupcakes. Trim the base to size. • Tie the ribbon over the cupcakes. Refer to the photograph.

CUPCAKES

1¼	cups (180 g) all-purpose (plain) flour	¾	cup (150 g) sugar
3	tablespoons unsweetened cocoa powder, sifted	½	teaspoon vanilla extract (essence)
		2	large eggs
1½	teaspoons baking powder	⅓	cup (90 ml) milk
		½	cup (125 g) fresh or frozen (thawed) strawberries
1	teaspoon ground cinnamon		
⅛	teaspoon salt	½	cup (90 g) dark chocolate chips
½	cup (125 g) unsalted butter, softened		

WHITE CHOCOLATE BUTTERCREAM

3	ounces (90 g) white chocolate	1	cup (150 g) confectioners' (icing) sugar
½	cup (125 g) unsalted butter, softened	⅛	teaspoon pink food coloring
¼	teaspoon vanilla extract (essence)		Confectionery hearts to decorate
½	tablespoon milk		

VALENTINE HEARTS CUPCAKES

Preheat the oven to 350°F (180°C/gas 4).
• Line a standard 12-cup muffin tin with paper liners. • **Cupcakes:** Combine the flour, cocoa, baking powder, cinnamon, and salt in a small bowl. • Beat the butter, sugar, and vanilla in a medium bowl with an electric mixer on medium-high speed until pale and creamy.
• Add the eggs one at a time, beating until just blended after each addition. • With mixer on low speed, add the mixed dry ingredients, alternating with the milk. • Stir the strawberries and chocolate chips in by hand. • Spoon the batter into the prepared cups, filling each one three-quarters full. • Bake for 20–25 minutes, until risen and firm to the touch. • Transfer the muffin tin to a wire rack. Let cool completely before removing the cupcakes. • **White Chocolate Buttercream:** Melt the chocolate in a double boiler over barely simmering water, stirring until smooth. Remove from the heat and let cool. • Beat the butter and vanilla in a medium bowl with an electric mixer on medium-high speed until pale and creamy.
• Pour in the milk and cooled chocolate, beating until blended. • Gradually add the confectioners' sugar, beating until blended.
• Tint pink with a few drops of pink food coloring. • Spoon the buttercream into a pastry bag fitted with a star shaped nozzle. Pipe a rosette on top of each cupcake and sprinkle with confectionery hearts.

MAKES: 12 PREPARATION: 40 MINUTES COOKING: 20–25 MINUTES LEVEL: 2

Cupcakes

1⅓ cups (200 g) all-purpose (plain) flour
⅓ cup (30 g) ground almonds
1½ teaspoons baking powder
⅛ teaspoon salt
1 cup (200 g) superfine (caster) sugar

2 large eggs
1 teaspoon finely grated orange zest
2 tablespoons orange-flower water
1 cup (250 ml) light (single) cream

To Decorate

1½ cups (225 g) confectioners' (icing) sugar
2 tablespoons water
⅛ teaspoon red food coloring
1 tablespoon unsweetened cocoa powder, sifted

BE MINE CUPCAKES

Preheat the oven to 350°F (180°C/gas 4).
• Line a standard 12-cup muffin tin with paper liners. • **Cupcakes:** Combine the flour, almonds, baking powder, and salt in a small bowl.
• Beat the sugar, eggs, and orange zest in a medium bowl with an electric mixer on medium-high speed until pale and creamy.
• With mixer on low speed, add the mixed dry ingredients, orange-flower water, and cream beating until just combined. • Spoon the batter into the prepared cups, filling each one three-quarters full. • Bake for 20–25 minutes, until golden brown and firm to the touch. • Transfer the muffin tin to a wire rack. Let cool completely before removing the cupcakes.
• Prepare a small paper piping bag: Cut a piece of parchment paper into an 8 x 12 x 14-inch (20 x 30 x 35-cm) triangle. Curl the paper into a cone-shape, forming the cone's point mid way along the long side. Tighten the cone and tuck the top flap inside the cone, securing with tape. • **To Decorate:** Combine the confectioners' sugar and water in a small bowl, stirring until smooth. Transfer a quarter of the mixture into a small bowl and tint pink with food coloring. Add the cocoa to the remaining frosting, plus a little extra water as needed and spread over the cupcakes. • Spoon the pink frosting into the prepared piping bag and cut off the end tip using scissors or a sharp knife. Pipe BE MINE on each cupcake.

MAKES: 12 PREPARATION: 45 MINUTES COOKING: 20–25 MINUTES LEVEL: 2

CUPCAKES

1	cup (150 g) all-purpose (plain) flour
2	teaspoons baking powder
⅛	teaspoon salt
½	cup (125 g) dairy-free spread

½	cup (100 g) sugar
1	teaspoon rose water
2	large eggs
¼	cup (60 ml) soy or oat milk
12	squares Turkish delight

TO DECORATE

1½	cups (225 g) confectioners' (icing) sugar
2	tablespoons water
⅛	teaspoon red food coloring

FOR MY SWEETHEART CUPCAKES

DAIRY FREE

Preheat the oven to 350°F (180°C/gas 4). • Line a standard 12-cup muffin tin with paper liners. • **Cupcakes:** Combine the flour, baking powder, and salt in a small bowl. • Beat the dairy-free spread, sugar, and rosewater in a medium bowl with an electric mixer on medium-high speed until creamy. • Add the eggs one at a time, beating until just blended after each addition. • With mixer on low speed, add the mixed dry ingredients, alternating with the milk. • Spoon the batter into the prepared cups, filling each one three-quarters full. • Press a square of Turkish delight into the top of each one. • Bake for 20–25 minutes, until golden brown and firm to the touch. • Transfer the muffin tin to a wire rack. Let cool completely before removing the cupcakes. • Prepare a small paper piping bag: Cut a piece of parchment paper into an 8 x 12 x 14-inch (20 x 30 x 35-cm) triangle. Curl the paper into a cone-shape, forming the cone's point mid way along the long side. Tighten the cone and tuck the top flap inside the cone, securing with tape. • **To Decorate:** Combine the confectioners' sugar and water in a small bowl, stirring until smooth. • Transfer a quarter of the mixture into a small bowl and tint red using a few drops of food coloring. • Spread the white frosting over the cupcakes. • Spoon the red frosting into the prepared piping bag and cut the tip off using scissors or a sharp knife. Pipe a few small hearts on top of each cupcake.

CUPCAKES				CHOCOLATE GANACHE		TO DECORATE	
12	ounces (350 g) dark chocolate	¼	cup (60 ml) maple syrup	4	ounces (120 g) dark chocolate, coarsely chopped	½	cup (75 g) confectioners' (icing) sugar
¾	cup (180 g) unsalted butter, chopped	1	cup (100 g) ground almonds	¼	cup (60 ml) light (single) cream	½	tablespoon water
6	large eggs	⅓	cup (50 g) flaked almonds, coarsely chopped			⅛	teaspoon pink food coloring
1	cup (200 g) firmly packed light brown sugar						

CHOCOLATE LOVE CUPCAKES

Preheat the oven to 325°F (170°C/gas 3).
• Line a 12-cup muffin pan with 10 paper liners.
Cupcakes: Melt the chocolate and butter in a double boiler over barely simmering water, stirring until smooth. Remove from the heat and let cool. • Beat the eggs, brown sugar, maple syrup, ground almonds, and flaked almonds in a medium bowl. • Pour in the chocolate and beat until combined. • Spoon the batter into the prepared cups, filling each one three-quarters full. • Bake for 25–30 minutes, until risen and firm to the touch.
• Transfer the muffin tin to a wire rack. Let cool completely before removing the cupcakes.
• Prepare a small paper piping bag: Cut a piece of parchment paper into an 8 x 12 x 14-inch (20 x 30 x 35-cm) triangle. Curl the paper into a cone-shape, forming the cone's point mid way along the long side. Tighten the cone and tuck the top flap inside the cone, securing with tape. • **Chocolate Ganache:** Melt the chocolate and cream in a double boiler over barely simmering water, stirring until smooth. Remove from the heat and let cool. • Spread the ganache over the cupcakes. • **To Decorate:** Combine the confectioners' sugar and water in a small bowl, stirring until smooth. Tint the frosting pink using a few drops of food coloring. • Spoon the frosting into the prepared piping bag and cut the tip off using scissors or a sharp knife. Pipe LOVE onto each of the cupcakes.

MAKES: 10 PREPARATION: 50 MINUTES COOKING: 25–30 MINUTES LEVEL: 2

CUPCAKES				TO DECORATE	
1¼	cups (180 g) all-purpose (plain) flour	1	teaspoon finely grated lemon zest	1½	cups (225 g) confectioners' (icing) sugar
1½	teaspoons baking powder	2	large eggs	2	tablespoons water
⅛	teaspoon salt	⅓	cup (90 ml) plain yogurt	⅛	teaspoon blue food coloring
½	cup (125 g) unsalted butter, softened	½	cup (125 g) fresh or frozen (thawed) blueberries	36	fresh blueberries
¾	cup (150 g) sugar				

LITTLE BOY BLUE MINI CUPCAKES

Preheat the oven to 350°F (180°C/gas 4).
• Line three 12-cup mini muffin pans with mini paper baking cups. • **Cupcakes:** Combine the flour, baking powder, and salt in a small bowl.
• Beat the butter, sugar, and lemon zest in a medium bowl with an electric mixer on medium-high speed until pale and creamy.
• Add the eggs one at a time, beating until just blended after each addition. • With mixer on low speed, add the mixed dry ingredients and yogurt. • Stir the blueberries in by hand. • Spoon the batter into the prepared cups, filling each one three-quarters full. • Bake for 15–20 minutes, until golden brown and firm to the touch. • Transfer the muffin tins to a wire rack. Let cool completely before removing the cupcakes. • Prepare a small paper piping bag:

Cut a piece of parchment paper into an 8 x 12 x 14-inch (20 x 30 x 35-cm) triangle. Curl the paper into a cone-shape, forming the cone's point mid way along the long side. Tighten the cone and tuck the top flap inside the cone, securing with tape. • **To Decorate:** Combine the confectioners' sugar and water in a small bowl, stirring until smooth. Tint the frosting bright blue with a few drops of food coloring. • Transfer a quarter of the mixture to a small bowl and add a few drops more drops of food coloring to create a darker blue frosting. • Spread the bright blue frosting over the cupcakes. • Spoon the dark blue frosting into the prepared piping bag and cut the tip off using scissors or a sharp knife.
• Pipe a border around each cupcake and place a blueberry in the center.

CUPCAKES

1¼ cups (180 g) all-purpose (plain) flour
1½ teaspoons baking powder
1 teaspoon ground cinnamon
⅛ teaspoon salt
½ cup (125 g) unsalted butter, softened

¾ cup (150 g) sugar
½ teaspoon vanilla extract (essence)
2 large eggs
⅓ cup (90 ml) milk
½ cup (125 g) fresh or frozen (thawed) strawberries

TO DECORATE

1½ cups (225 g) confectioners' (icing) sugar
2 tablespoons water
⅛ teaspoon red food coloring
36 pink jelly beans or candy coated buttons

PRETTY IN PINK MINI CUPCAKES

Preheat the oven to 350°F (180°C/gas 4).
• Line three 12-cup mini muffin pans with mini paper baking cups. • Combine the flour, baking powder, cinnamon, and salt in a small bowl.
• Beat the butter, sugar, and vanilla in a medium bowl with an electric mixer on medium-high speed until pale and creamy.
• Add the eggs one at a time, beating until just blended after each addition. • With mixer on low speed, add the mixed dry ingredients, alternating with the milk. • Stir the strawberries in by hand. • Spoon the batter into the prepared cups, filling each one three-quarters full. • Bake for 15–20 minutes, until golden brown and firm to the touch. • Transfer the muffin tins to a wire rack. Let cool completely before removing the cupcakes. • Prepare a small paper piping bag: Cut a piece of parchment paper into an 8 x 12 x 14-inch (20 x 30 x 35-cm) triangle. Curl the paper into a cone-shape, forming the cone's point mid way along the long side. Tighten the cone and tuck the top flap inside the cone, securing with tape. • **To Decorate:** Combine the confectioners' sugar and water in a small bowl, stirring until smooth. Tint the frosting light pink with a few drops of food coloring. • Transfer a quarter of the mixture to a small bowl and add a few more drops of red food coloring to create a dark pink frosting. • Spread the light pink frosting over the cupcakes. • Spoon the dark pink frosting into the prepared piping bag and cut the tip off using scissors or a sharp knife.
• Pipe a border around each cupcake and place a jellybean or candy-coated button in the center.

MAKES: 36 PREPARATION: 45 MINUTES COOKING: 15–20 MINUTES LEVEL: 2

CUPCAKES

1¼ cups (180 g) all-purpose (plain) flour
½ teaspoon baking powder
¼ teaspoon baking soda (bicarbonate of soda)
⅛ teaspoon salt
2 large eggs
1 cup (200 g) sugar

1 teaspoon vanilla extract (essence)
½ cup (125 ml) vegetable oil
½ cup (125 ml) soy or oat milk
½ cup (125 g) mixed fresh or frozen (thawed) raspberries or blueberries

CITRUS FROSTING

2 cups (300 g) confectioners' (icing) sugar
2 tablespoons orange juice, strained
1 tablespoon freshly squeezed lemon juice, strained

TO DECORATE

12 mini novelty cupid dolls

BABY DOLL CUPCAKES

Preheat the oven to 325°F (170°C/gas 3). • Line two 12-cup muffin pans with 18 paper liners. • **Cupcakes:** Combine the flour, baking powder, baking soda, and salt in a small bowl. • Beat the eggs, sugar, and vanilla in a medium bowl with an electric mixer on medium-high speed until pale and creamy. • With mixer on low speed, add the mixed dry ingredients, oil, and milk. • Fold the berries in by hand. • Spoon the batter into the prepared cups, filling each one three-quarters full. • Bake for 25–30 minutes, until golden brown and firm to the touch. • Transfer the muffin tins to a wire rack. Let cool completely before removing the cupcakes. • **Citrus Frosting:** Combine the confectioners' sugar and orange and lemon juice in a small bowl, stirring until smooth. • Spread the frosting over the cupcakes and place a novelty doll on top of each one.

MAKES: 18 PREPARATION: 35 MINUTES COOKING: 25–30 MINUTES LEVEL: 1

CUPCAKES

3 ounces (90 g) white chocolate, coarsely chopped
⅓ cup (90 ml) light (single) cream
¾ cup (150 g) all-purpose (plain) flour
½ cup (50 g) ground pistachios

1 teaspoon baking powder
⅛ teaspoon salt
⅓ cup (90 g) unsalted butter, softened
1 cup (200 g) sugar
½ teaspoon vanilla extract (essence)
2 large eggs

CHOCOLATE FROSTING

½ cup (125 g) unsalted butter, softened
½ teaspoon vanilla extract (essence)
1⅓ cups (200 g) confectioners' (icing) sugar
2½ tablespoons unsweetened cocoa powder, sifted
½ tablespoon water

TO DECORATE

3½ ounces (100 g) ready-to-use fondant
Confectioners' (icing) sugar, to dust
Thin purple colored ribbon

SCROLL CERTIFICATE CUPCAKES

Preheat the oven to 325°F (170°C/gas 3). • Line a standard 12-cup muffin tin with paper liners. **Cupcakes:** Melt the chocolate and cream in a double boiler over barely simmering water, stirring until smooth. Remove from the heat and let cool. • Combine the flour, pistachios, baking powder, and salt in a small bowl. • Beat the butter, sugar, and vanilla in a medium bowl with an electric mixer on medium-high speed until pale and creamy. • Add the eggs one at a time, beating until just blended after each addition. • With mixer on low speed, add the mixed dry ingredients and melted chocolate. • Spoon the batter into the prepared cups, filling each one three-quarters full. • Bake for

25–30 minutes, until risen and firm to the touch. • Transfer the muffin tin to a wire rack. Let cool completely before removing the cupcakes. • **Chocolate Frosting:** Beat the butter and vanilla in a small bowl using an electric mixer until creamy. • Gradually add the confectioners' sugar, cocoa, and water, beating until combined. Spread the frosting over the cupcakes. • **To Decorate:** Dust a clean work surface with confectioners' sugar and knead the fondant until smooth. • Roll out to ⅛ inch (3 mm) thick. • Cut out twelve ¾ x 1½-inch (2 x 4-cm) rectangles. Roll up to resemble scrolls and tie pieces of ribbon around the center. Place on top of the cupcakes.

MAKES: 12 PREPARATION: 45 MINUTES COOKING: 25–30 MINUTES LEVEL: 2

Cupcakes

2 cups (300 g) all-purpose (plain) flour
¼ cup (30 g) unsweetened cocoa powder
2 teaspoons baking powder
1 teaspoon baking soda (bicarbonate of soda)
⅛ teaspoon salt
½ cup (125 ml) vegetable oil
1½ cups (325 ml) maple syrup
1 cup (250 ml) water
1 teaspoon vanilla extract (essence)

White Chocolate Ganache

4 ounces (120 g) white chocolate, coarsely chopped
¼ cup (60 ml) light (single) cream

To Decorate

1 piece log (round) liquorice
Strap liquorice
1 tube black frosting

GRADUATION HAT CUPCAKES

Preheat the oven to 350°F (180°C/gas 4).
• Line a standard 12-cup muffin tin with paper liners. • **Cupcakes:** Combine the flour, cocoa, baking powder, baking soda, and salt in a medium bowl. • Combine the oil, maple syrup, water, and vanilla in a medium bowl. • Pour the liquid mixture into the mixed dry ingredients and stir until combined. Do not over mix.
• Spoon the batter into the prepared cups, filling each one three-quarters full. • Bake for 15–20 minutes, until risen and firm to the touch.
• Transfer the muffin tin to a wire rack. Let cool completely before removing the cupcakes.
White Chocolate Ganache: Melt the chocolate and cream in a double boiler over barely simmering water, stirring until smooth. Remove from the heat and let cool. • Spread the ganache over the cupcakes. • **To Decorate:** Cut the liquorice log into twelve rounds, for the base of the hat. Cut twelve squares of strap liquorice for the top of the hat. Cut twenty-four thin short strips out of the strap liquorice, to use for the tassels of the hats. • Add a tip to the black frosting tube and pipe a small dot of the frosting in the center of each liquorice square and stick on two thin strips. Let set. • Pipe another dot of frosting in the center of the liquorice rounds.
• Place the squares on top at an angle to create a graduation hat. Place the hats on the cupcakes, securing with a little frosting.

CUPCAKES

3¼ cups (480 g) coconut milk powder
4 cups (600 g) all-purpose (plain) flour
4 teaspoons baking powder
½ teaspoon salt

2 cups (500 g) unsalted butter, softened
4 cup (800 g) sugar
4 teaspoons vanilla extract (essence)
16 large eggs

CHOCOLATE GANACHE

1 pound (500 g) dark chocolate, coarsely chopped
1 cup (250 ml) light (single) cream

TO DECORATE

12 ounces (350 g) white chocolate, coarsely chopped
Gold leaf

GOLDEN JUBILEE CUPCAKES

Preheat the oven to 325°F (170°C/gas 3).
• Line four standard 12-cup muffin tins with gold lined baking cups. • **Cupcakes:** Combine the coconut milk powder, flour, baking powder, and salt in a large bowl. • Beat the butter, sugar, and vanilla in a large bowl with an electric mixer on medium-high speed until pale and creamy. • Add the eggs one at a time, beating until just blended after each addition. • With mixer on low speed, add the mixed dry ingredients. • Spoon the batter into the prepared cups, filling each one three-quarters full. • Bake in batches for 25–30 minutes, until golden brown and firm to the touch. • Transfer the muffin tins to a wire rack. Let cool completely before removing the cupcakes.

Chocolate Ganache: Melt the chocolate and cream in a double boiler over barely simmering water, stirring until smooth. Remove from the heat and let cool and thicken. • Spread over the top of the cupcakes. • **To Decorate:** Melt the white chocolate in a double boiler over barely simmering water, stirring until smooth. Remove from the heat and let cool. • Pour the chocolate onto a clean glass, marble, or stainless steel surface and allow to set. • Create chocolate curls using a small knife. • Pile chocolate curls on top of the cupcakes and flake gold leaf on top.

CUPCAKES

3 cups **(500 g) mixed dried fruit**
1 cup **(250 g) unsalted butter, cubed**
1¾ cups **(350 g) firmly packed light brown sugar**
3 **large eggs, lightly beaten**

1 teaspoon **vanilla extract (essence)**
½ teaspoon **almond extract (essence)**
2½ cups **(375 g) all-purpose (plain) flour**
1 teaspoon **baking powder**
¼ teaspoon **salt**

TO DECORATE

1 cup **(150 g) confectioners' (icing) sugar**
4 pounds **(2 kg) ready-to-use white fondant**
1 cup **(325 g) orange marmalade, warmed and strained**

1½ teaspoons **silver lustre**
1½ teaspoons **vodka**
Silver ribbon
Small white fondant or sugar flowers

SILVER CUPCAKES

Preheat the oven to 350°F (180°C/gas 4). • Line three standard 12-cup muffin tin with 32 paper liners. • **Cupcakes:** Combine the fruit in a medium saucepan and cover with water. Bring to a boil on medium heat and simmer for 5 minutes. • Drain and return the fruit to the pan. • Stir in the butter until melted. • Add the brown sugar, eggs, and vanilla and almond extracts, stirring until combined. • Combine the flour, baking powder, and salt in a medium bowl and add to the fruit mixture, stirring until combined. • Spoon the batter into the prepared cups, filling each one three-quarters full. • Bake for 20–25 minutes, until golden brown and firm to the touch. • Transfer the muffin tins to a wire rack. Let cool completely before removing the cupcakes. • **To Decorate:** Dust a clean work surface with confectioners' sugar and knead the fondant until smooth. Roll out to ¼ inch (5 mm) thick. • Cut out rounds, using a small sharp knife, big enough to cover the entire cupcakes. • Remove the papers from the cupcakes and brush with marmalade. Place the fondant rounds on top. Smooth over the edges and trim the base to size. • Combine the silver lustre and vodka in a small bowl. Using a small paint brush, paint the flowers with lustre and leave to dry. • Tie the ribbon around the middle of each cupcake, finishing off with a bow. Decorate with the flowers. • Refer to the photograph.

MAKES: 32 PREPARATION: 1 HOUR 30 MINUTES COOKING: 25–20 MINUTES LEVEL: 3

276

Cupcakes

- 1⅓ cups (200 g) all-purpose (plain) flour
- ⅓ cup (30 g) ground almonds
- 2 teaspoons baking powder
- ⅛ teaspoon salt
- ½ cup (125 g) unsalted butter, softened
- ½ cup (100 g) sugar
- 2 teaspoons finely grated orange zest
- 2 large eggs
- ⅓ cup (90 ml) sour cream
- 3 tablespoons freshly squeezed orange juice, strained

To Decorate

- ½ cup (75 g) confectioners' (icing) sugar
- 14 ounces (400 g) ready-to-use white fondant
- ⅓ cup (100 g) orange marmalade, warmed and strained
- 12 confectionery gold coins
- 3½ feet (1.5 m) royal blue ribbon
- 1 ounce (30 g) white chocolate, melted

BEST IN SHOW CUPCAKES

Preheat the oven to 350°F (180°C/gas 4).
• Line a standard 12-cup muffin tin with paper liners. • **Cupcakes:** Combine the flour, almonds, baking powder, and salt in a small bowl. • Beat the butter, sugar, and orange zest in a medium bowl with an electric mixer on medium-high speed until pale and creamy. • Add the eggs one at a time, beating until just blended after each addition. • With mixer on low speed, add the mixed dry ingredients, sour cream, and orange juice. • Spoon the batter into the prepared cups, filling each one three-quarters full. • Bake for 20–25 minutes, until golden brown and firm to the touch. • Transfer the muffin tin to a wire rack. Let cool completely before removing the cupcakes. • **To Decorate:** Dust a clean work surface with confectioners' sugar and knead the fondant until smooth.
• Roll out to ¼ inch (5 mm) thick. • Using a cookie cutter or glass, cut out rounds big enough to cover the tops of the cupcakes.
• Brush the cupcakes with marmalade and place the fondant rounds on top. • Cut the ribbon into twenty-four 2-inch (5-cm) lengths. Use the ribbon and gold coins to create a first place medal on top of the cupcakes. Use melted chocolate to stick the ribbon and hold in place.

MAKES: 12 PREPARATION: 1 HOUR COOKING: 20–25 MINUTES LEVEL: 3

CUPCAKES

- ½ cup (60 g) amaranth flour
- ¾ cup (125 g) rice flour
- 1 tablespoon (8 g) xanthan gum
- 1 teaspoon baking soda (bicarbonate of soda)
- 1 teaspoon ground cinnamon
- ¼ teaspoon ground cloves
- ⅛ teaspoon salt

- 2 large eggs
- ¾ cup (150 g) sugar
- ½ cup (125 ml) vegetable oil
- ¼ cup (60 ml) water
- ¾ cup (135 g) tart apple, such as Granny Smith or Greening, peeled, cored, and finely chopped
- ½ cup (60 g) walnuts, coarsely chopped

CREAM CHEESE FROSTING

- ⅔ cup (150 g) cream cheese, softened
- ½ teaspoon finely grated lemon zest
- ⅔ cup (100 g) confectioners' (icing) sugar
- 1 tablespoon freshly squeezed lemon juice, strained

  Sugar flowers, to decorate

MOTHER'S DAY CUPCAKES

Preheat the oven to 325°F (170°C/gas 3).
• Line a standard 12-cup muffin tin with paper liners. • **Cupcakes:** Combine both flours, xanthan gum, baking soda, cinnamon, cloves, and salt in a medium bowl. • Whisk the eggs in a medium bowl with an electric mixer on medium-high speed until frothy. • Add the sugar, oil, and water and whisk until incorporated. • With mixer on low speed, add the mixed dry ingredients. • Stir in the apple and walnuts by hand. • Spoon the batter into the prepared cups, filling each one three-quarters full. • Bake for 25–30 minutes, until golden brown and firm to the touch. • Transfer the muffin tin to a wire rack. Let cool completely before removing the cupcakes.
• **Cream Cheese Frosting:** Beat the cream cheese and lemon zest in a small bowl using an electric mixer on medium speed until creamy.
• Add the confectioners' sugar, and lemon juice, beating until combined. • Spread the frosting on each cupcake. Top with the flowers.

66 *Add a special touch to these cupcakes by wrapping the finished cakes in a pretty decorative paper.*

MAKES: 12   PREPARATION: 45 MINUTES   COOKING: 25–30 MINUTES   LEVEL: 1

CUPCAKES

3 ounces (90 g) dark chocolate
⅓ cup (90 ml) light (single) cream
1 cup (150 g) all-purpose (plain) flour
2 tablespoons unsweetened cocoa powder, sifted
1 teaspoon baking powder
⅛ teaspoon salt
⅓ cup (90 g) unsalted butter, softened
1 cup (200 g) sugar
2 large eggs
2 tablespoons cherry brandy
½ cup (125 g) drained maraschino cherries, coarsely chopped

CHOCOLATE GANACHE

4 ounces (120 g) dark chocolate
¼ cup (60 ml) light (single) cream

TO DECORATE

½ cup (75 g) confectioners' (icing) sugar
½ tablespoon water

FATHER'S DAY CUPCAKES

Preheat the oven to 350°F (180°C/gas 4).
• Line a standard 12-cup muffin tin with paper liners. • **Cupcakes:** Melt the chocolate and cream in a double boiler over barely simmering water, stirring until smooth. Remove from the heat and let cool. • Combine the flour, cocoa, baking powder, and salt in a small bowl. • Beat the butter and sugar in a medium bowl with an electric mixer on medium-high speed until pale and creamy. • Add the eggs one at a time, beating until just blended after each addition. • With mixer on low speed, add the mixed dry ingredients, melted chocolate, and cherry brandy. • Stir in the cherries by hand. • Spoon the batter into the prepared cups, filling each one three-quarters full. • Bake for 20–25 minutes, until risen and firm to the touch. • Transfer the muffin tin to a wire rack. Let

cool completely before removing the cupcakes.
• Prepare a small paper piping bag: Cut a piece of parchment paper into an 8 x 12 x 14-inch (20 x 30 x 35-cm) triangle. Curl the paper into a cone-shape, forming the cone's point mid way along the long side. Tighten the cone and tuck the top flap inside the cone, securing with tape. • **Chocolate Ganache:** Melt the chocolate and cream in a double boiler over barely simmering water, stirring until smooth. Remove from the heat and let cool and thicken.
• Spread over the cupcakes. • **To Decorate:** Combine the confectioners' sugar and water in a small bowl, stirring until smooth. • Spoon the white frosting into the prepared piping bag and cut the tip off using scissors or a sharp knife.
• Pipe DAD or WORLD'S BEST DAD on top of each cupcake.

MAKES: 12 PREPARATION: 30 MINUTES COOKING: 20–25 MINUTES LEVEL: 2

index

INDEX

286